MOOD MAGICK

Wellness Spells & Rituals to Find Balance in an Uncertain World

ORA NORTH

REVEAL PRESS

AN IMPRINT OF NEW HARBINGER PUBLICATIONS

Distributed in Canada by Raincoast Books

NEW HARBINGER PUBLICATIONS is a registered trademark of New Harbinger Publications, Inc.

Copyright © 2022 by Ora North
Reveal Press
An imprint of New Harbinger Publications, Inc.
5674 Shattuck Avenue
Oakland, CA 94609
www.newharbinger.com

Cover design by Sara Christian

Cover illustration by Saydung89

Interior design by Michele Waters-Kermes

Acquired by Jennye Garibaldi

Edited by Diedre Hammons

All Rights Reserved

FSC
www.fsc.org
MIX
Paper from
responsible sources
FSC® C011935

Library of Congress Cataloging-in-Publication Data

Names: North, Ora, author.
Title: Mood magick : wellness spells and rituals to find balance in an uncertain world / Ora North.
Description: Oakland, CA : New Harbinger Publications, [2022]
Identifiers: LCCN 2021036238 | ISBN 9781684038909 (trade paperback)
Subjects: LCSH: Witchcraft. | Magic.
Classification: LCC BF1566 .N67 2022 | DDC 133.4/46--dc23
LC record available at https://lccn.loc.gov/2021036238

Printed in the United States of America

24   23   22

10   9   8   7   6   5   4   3   2   1   First Printing

"Many of the clients I work with are looking for new and alternative exercises they can integrate into their life to help them feel more connected to themselves and the world around them. Ora North's book, *Mood Magick*, guides readers through beautifully conscious activities that can help them to ground back into their life using the world that is naturally surrounding them."

> —**Elizabeth Earnshaw, LMFT**, owner of A Better Life Therapy, therapist at Actually, and author of *I Want This to Work*

"YES! Finally, a book on magic that implements the most important aspect of our existence: the human body and everything that comes with that. I believe this is the one and only way to being successful in life, and Ora did an extraordinary job in writing this amazing book: clear, hands-on, and magical. A must-have!"

> —**Bara Cerna/Soviet Mercedes**, money witch, demon whisperer, and international dominatrix

"We are living through one of the most pivotal chapters in the more-than-human story. Now, more than ever, we need practices and poetry that remind us that magick is not only real, but the very medicine necessary for the disconnection that ails us. Ora North eloquently offers medicinal 'mood' magick as an accessible and timely remedy to many of the common ills of modernity, and, to that end, this book is absolutely an essential read."

> —**Danielle Dulsky**, author of *The Holy Wild*, *Seasons of Moon and Flame*, and *The Sacred Hags Oracle*

"Ora has delivered yet another powerful book that offers earth-based wisdom and a concrete set of practices for those seeking to create safety, steadiness, and sustainability in our overwhelming world. I will highly recommend this book and its empowering rituals to my clients as a foundation to their mental health and spiritual wellness routines."

> —**Pamela Kowal, MS, LMFT**, licensed marriage and family therapist, integrative psychotherapist, and soul mentor

"Ora North's beautifully written book, *Mood Magick*, is a unique compendium of spells and rituals for novice and advanced magickal practitioners. I'm grateful North's book is geared to readers with mental health challenges, especially since I have bipolar disorder. Yet, *Mood Magick* benefits anyone interested in exploring simple, powerful, elemental magick. North inspires one to reengage with life through thoughtfully designed witchcraft ranging from grounding and healing to creativity and passion. *Mood Magick* is a brilliant, innovative work!"

—**Dyane Harwood**, author of *Birth of a New Brain*

"Ora North has done it again—like her last book, *I Don't Want to Be an Empath Anymore, Mood Magick* is an instant classic. It's grounded, accessible, kind, and written for the spirit of the times—how to take care of ourselves in a world that often overwhelms us with information, sensory input, and unprecedented responsibilities for our survival. Anyone can benefit from integrating these rituals and practices into their everyday lives."

—**Arden Leigh**, creator of The Re-Patterning Project, and frontwoman of Arden & the Wolves

"*Mood Magick* tackles the thorny problem of mental health and magick when the world is filled with anxiety and uncertainty. Ora's teachings are openhearted and practical, grounded in esoteric philosophy while being accessible and fun. These are bits of wisdom we should all learn when growing up to navigate the difficulties of life, but few of us do. Use the teaching of *Mood Magick* to find an ever-shifting balance in these challenging times."

—**Christopher Penczak**, author of the *Temple of Witchcraft* series; *The Casting of Spells*; and *Buddha, Christ, Merlin*

Contents

Introduction

Witches have captured our imaginations for hundreds of years as wildly varying archetypes of healers, monsters, empowered feminists, evildoers, chosen ones, and mystics. Being able to span such a contradictory spectrum of morality proves just how powerful the archetype of the witch really is, even if we can't seem to nail down one solid definition or character. The witch's prevalence also hints at how accessible the power of the witch is to all of us, even if we can't quite figure out how to approach it.

For the purpose of this book, I describe witches as those who have a special connection to the elements of nature and choose to harness the elements' powers and energies to understand the world and to create change. Witches are elemental philosophers with a scientist's curiosity to understand and then apply. Although there are many different types of witches who focus on certain elements, practices, or deities, their goal—transformation—is the same. Witches can have a solitary practice or practice with a group, often called a coven. There are many intricate hierarchies and training groups for witchcraft, but you don't need to be in a formal coven to use the tenets of witchcraft to improve your life and create peace and wellness. Wherever you're starting from is the perfect place to start.

The one thing that most people can agree on when it comes to the witch archetype is that the witch uses magick. How people perceive magick is often how they define what a witch is, and this is where some can get really hung up on concern or fear. I would ask that if you feel any resistance or fear of magick, keep an open mind to what I'm about to tell you: magick may not be what you think it is.

Magick is a far more intimate and imaginative art than simply conjuring spells or calling upon spirits. More than anything else, the practice of ritual is a psychological practice, similar to meditation, prayer, poetry, or therapy. Ritual encourages you to reflect on your feelings and creatively make physical symbols of those internal feelings and experiences, thus connecting what's inside of you to what's outside of you in the world. This not only integrates your inner and outer worlds but it also creates a deeper understanding of your purpose and place in the world as both a spiritual being and a physical being. It's the basis of the magickal phrases "As above, so below" and "As within, so without."

Magick is metaphor made real. It's feeling our sadness as water and pouring a chalice into the earth to represent the grounding of our feelings into stability. It's the realization that if we lack passion, we can light a candle and work with the flame to reignite our hearts. It's a practice of imagination, creativity, and spirit. Magick allows us to tell stories, even in very small ways, that connect us to our bodies and our internal worlds. By creating symbols of our feelings and experiences in our internal worlds and bringing them into the physical world through ritual, we bring those metaphors to life. We create magick. We shift the way we interact with the world, and in turn, the way the world interacts with us.

Given the unlimited source of creativity that this opens up, you may have noticed witchcraft as a growing trend. As the seasons change without fail, so does the adaptability of witchery. The social activist witch. The feminist witch. The political witch. Complicated modern issues call for the simplicity, power, and transformation of witchcraft, and we can adapt those simple elemental forces to anything we desire. As mental health comes to the forefront of our cultural landscape in our ever-changing world, we can adapt those forces to become mood witches as well.

The Decline of Mental Health

We can always rely on change as our one constant in modern life. Change of information, change of approach, change of policy, change of how we function and interact. It all happens so quickly. Information flies at us a million times faster than we can absorb or implement even a small portion of it. Phones and computers are constantly pinging us with notifications, both personal and work-related. Detailed and repeated coverage of tragedies like mass shootings, pandemics, climate change, and other global and cultural crises consume our nervous systems.

The speed and overstimulation of information streams, unfortunately, contribute to a decline in overall mental health as our awareness of a complicated world grows and grows without the tools to keep ourselves steady within it. Social media consumption and online harassment only increase as our dependence on the online world to achieve creative expression, personal validation, and business success increases as well. Because so much of this takes place in the digital world, our connection to the physical and natural world fades and we have no choice but to rely on this supercharged information stream for safety and stability. Of course, this information stream can only promise change and instability, so we find ourselves looking for stability in the most unstable of places. If you already suffer from anxiety, manic highs, or obsessive tendencies, this paralyzing mental overload can exacerbate and trigger your symptoms and episodes all too easily, creating a vicious cycle of instability that feels impossible to step out of.

Making it even harder to step out of this cycle, we feel that in order to stay informed, to keep up, to survive, or to contribute, we must constantly stay within those information streams. Our focus is divided among hundreds of things in the supercharged digital world, most of which we are powerless to do anything about. In times of the past, before the Age of Information, the pace was much slower and the mind had more space to focus on fewer things at a time. Yes, the access to information that we now have is amazing. Yes, we are able to learn about things we never would have had the opportunity to otherwise.

But also, the mind was not meant to process data like a computer. The mind was meant to linger and ponder, to develop and connect, to evolve at a more sustainable pace. Who now has the time or mental space to stare at the veins of a leaf for an hour, realizing that they echo the rivers crossing the globe in a vast network of living systems? Who now is allowed to freely drop their responsibilities in a claustrophobic world for a few hours to feel the warm sand on their toes, twirling them slowly until they truly understand the microcosm beneath their feet? Creating magick requires focus, and these types of simple, focused activities are naturally infused with power. The practices in this book will lead you away from overstimulation and back into simplicity.

If overstimulation of the mind is the first condition that contributes to the overall decline of mental health, losing the connection to our physical bodies is the second. Spending so much time in the informational realm makes it harder to inhabit the physical one, which can feel like being out of sync with your body or feeling like you're not even fully in it. Physical sensations may be dull or distant, and the primal pleasures that one experiences like eating, movement, and sex may be absent. If you're not in your body, not only are you missing out on those pleasures but you are also not fully connected to your innate wisdom and intuition, which only feeds the negative effects of overstimulation. We need our physical bodies to help us process our mental energy. When we're disconnected from the body, all the excess energy of the mind doesn't have a place to ground and stabilize.

If you struggle with your mental health or have a history of trauma that causes you to dissociate or disconnect from your body as a measure of protection, the lack of connection to the physical world already present for everyone can amplify those traumatic experiences and make it even harder for you to connect into the life you want to live. Rituals and spells can easily be altered to adjust for dissociation so you can go at your own pace in a way that slowly helps you connect with your body rather than re-traumatize you by making large jumps. By taking small pieces of the rituals or only focusing on one element at a time, you can gradually create a safer space in your outer world for your internal world experiences. Creating those safe spaces is especially important for those who are neurodivergent, who have a very different lived experience than the neurotypical. Having such a different lived experience creates an even bigger gap between your inner world and outer world, especially when the outer world isn't keen on accepting or working with your unique inner world.

If your mental health struggles involve an intense racing mind that fills your head with information like a light bulb with too much wattage, the lack of physical connection can make that light bulb crack or break. If you imagined all that mental stimulation like electricity in the brain, without a lightning rod to pull it down into the ground, you can easily see how even situational anxiety would grow to the point where we couldn't regulate it at all. Without a connection to the physical body, there is no connection to the physical earth. Losing touch with that connection easily creates mental imbalances because it thrusts us onto a path that's not natural for us to be on. We need the physical world to regulate our nervous systems, and also so we can experience joy and pleasure.

Witchcraft is the practice that can be the lightning rod, grounding our excess mental energies and connecting us back into our bodies so we can live a fuller, more stable, and more peaceful life.

The Four Elements

The basic practice of witchcraft is working with the four elements: earth, water, fire, and air. Each element has universal symbolism and themes, though they can be amplified and customized based on your personal connection to them. Each element can be tied to different mental states and moods.

Earth is the grounding, the stabilizing, the safety. It's the old oak tree that has stood strong and watched hundreds of years of history move past it. It's the sand on the beach that's pushed and pulled with the tides, but always remains. It's the cemetery that holds the bones of our ancestors so we can remember where we came from. It's also the landslide that buries and destroys with bold, stubborn force.

Water is the washing, the cleansing, the soothing. It is the deep and still pool, holding us in silence like a comforting womb. It is the stormy sea, carrying the strength of our emotions across the distance. It is the graceful stream, showing us how our lives can flow with such elegance. It's also the raging flood, showing us how destructive the rush of our rawness can be.

Fire is the burning, the sparking, the transforming. It's the steady burn that encourages our survival. It is the beautiful firework that inspires us to ooh and ahh. It's the candlelight that ignites our passions and sensuality. It is the transforming of matter to ash to matter again, the destruction and rebirth. It is also the spontaneous wildfire that spreads without reason or care, burning all in its path.

Air is the moving, the thinking, the acting. It's the gentle breeze running its fingers through your hair as it whispers lovely secrets to you. It's the very force that allows the fire to blaze, sparking brilliance and genius ideas. It's the cyclone that surrounds you in the eye of the storm, bringing you all the information you could possibly want to move forward. It's also the cold and bitter wind that bites at your senses and prevents you from moving at all.

Because our entire existence can be traced back to the elements, using the elements is the perfect way to connect your inner world experiences to a tangible physical world, thus bridging the gap and creating the change you seek. Working with the elements to create magick is nothing new to anyone, even if you aren't aware of it yet. Our bodies are made up of the elements, and they perform magick on a daily basis. Your body is itself made of earth, and it recycles itself both in life and in death. You are primarily water, and your blood flows through you like a river with purpose. Your neurons fire and crackle in your brain, creating electrical pathways like fireworks and lightning. Your lungs expand and contract with the air you breathe. Every element relies on every other element, and together, they interact with one another and keep you alive. Each element also has its own emotional and spiritual meaning, and by using the elements as guideposts for symbols and metaphors, we can connect to our own bodies and to the body of the earth to balance our emotional, spiritual, and physical worlds. We can understand ourselves better and create shifts in how we experience both.

Working with the elements in their simplest forms is often overlooked because of the overstimulating information stream and how that information speed has changed our cultural values. By being in that energy of constantly trying to keep up with the impossible speed of new and changing information, we set up the expectation that speed and efficiency in all matters is king. That becomes what we value. That obsession with speed puts us at odds with nature. Nature has its own rhythms, and they are entirely separate from the rhythms of the digital world. We can try to superimpose the digital rhythm onto the natural world, but then we find ourselves hiking to the top of the mountain as quickly and efficiently as possible, without slowing down to observe the natural world and the life-affirming lessons it offers. This tendency is more about conquering nature than working with it.

To get back to the basics, we need to shift our lenses from conquering nature to working with it. By seeing how the rhythm of the digital world simply doesn't translate to the rhythm of the natural world, we can begin to separate the two. We can work with the rhythm of the natural world in both our bodies and in our external environments, rather than trying to go against it or over it. To begin to flow with nature again, we can do the simple work of communing with the four elements, and in doing so, access the powers of those elements as additional mental health tools. This is a journey back to simplicity, to a slower pace, to presence.

In this book, you'll discover how to connect with those four elements. You'll learn the ways you're already connected to them and you'll learn how to perform simple spells and rituals that will help you ground, find mental stability, and create peace of mind that will have a ripple effect throughout your entire life.

You don't need to be advanced in these practices by any means to get results. These rituals are meant to meet you where you're at, even if you've never dabbled in magick before. You'll even be able to customize them in order for them to feel more meaningful and personal to you. With everything that I share, I always encourage you to take what is helpful for you and discard the rest. There are no hard and fast rules since your mental health needs are constantly changing with the changing world. I have bipolar disorder and a history of trauma, so these practices have helped to serve as my lightning rod, giving me a safe grounded space to both process my lived experiences touched by mental illness and develop and strengthen my power and pleasure in the world. It is in that spirit that I share them with you.

I also want to stress that none of this work is meant to replace the care of a licensed doctor or medical professional. Witchcraft is just one additional tool you can add to your preexisting toolbox. Practicing ritual does not exclude other mental health tools such as therapy, medication, psychiatry, habits in nutrition, movement, and sleep. You get to make the rules on what works for you and what doesn't, and I encourage you to use every tool you have at your disposal. A holistic view is a whole view, and working with the elements encourages a balance in everything.

CHAPTER 1

Grounding and Intention

Two practices need to be done before any ritual work can take hold: grounding and setting intention. Grounding sets the stage so you're in the best place to give and receive energy in a balanced and healthy way, and setting your intention for your rituals ensures that the energy and magick you call upon is moving in the way you desire it to. These practices should be done before each ritual or spell, but they're also great practices for daily life whether you're actively practicing magick or not.

Grounding

Grounding, also called *earthing,* is when your biomagnetic field connects to and interacts with the earth's electromagnetic field. By allowing your body to physically connect with the earth, balance and stability are created on both a physical and spiritual level and can simultaneously help ease pain on each level.

On an energetic level, many forms of mental imbalance and anxiety are caused by excess energy in your upper body and your mind, complicated by energetic blockages in your lower body. This keeps you from naturally moving that upper mental energy down through your lower body and into the earth to keep you grounded in the physical world. When you are disconnected from the earth in this way, you could panic, become manic, or lose your sense of self. Grounding is your first defense when it comes to disconnection from your body.

Many of us avoid grounding because we associate connecting with our bodies to connecting with the stresses of daily reality. We consider those realities to be the external world, so we may consciously or unconsciously avoid them. But, the external world is not just the gears of modern life and the stress it causes. The external world is the physical body of the Divine. It's the power of the elements and nature, completely independent from human involvement and civilization, following cycles and rules all of its own. It can be seen as a macrocosmic representation of your own physical body. Using this perspective, we can reframe what we consider our outer world of the patriarchy-driven infrastructures that make you feel unsupported and stressed out to the natural order of nature and its ability to move and exist in a much different way.

Since our bodies are simply micro-versions of the earth, we need to be connected into the vast network of the land and the natural order to feel supported outside of those patriarchal hierarchies. This becomes increasingly clear as we struggle to adjust to a constantly changing world where our very earth is at stake, threatening the very foundation of our safety. On top of that, technology and social media keep so much of our energy up in the mind and idea realm that it becomes even harder to naturally reach that place of groundedness. These subtleties and complications only emphasize the importance of reframing what we consider the outer world and establishing an intentional grounding practice.

Practicing grounding, even in incredibly unstable times, is the most effective way to connect us to that network and make us feel safe and stable in our bodies—and it can immediately ease anxiety and frenetic energy. This is the reason I'd consider earth to be the most important element in mental health magick. If you were only to do one single thing from this book, I would hope it is the practice of grounding.

It's important to note that grounding can be a difficult practice if you've experienced trauma that has caused you to dissociate from your body. Sometimes, intentionally coming back into your body can be scary and triggering. If this is the case, make sure to approach grounding exercises with care, and take it slow.

Here are a few grounding exercises you can easily use in your practice.

SIMPLE GROUNDING FOR EVERYDAY STABILITY

This grounding exercise can be used for any ritual or any reason. It's wonderful as a daily practice with or without ritual work afterward.

You need bare feet for this exercise. Find a spot outside that feels good to you. Maybe the beach is your favorite spot and you can stick your toes in the sand. Maybe the forest is your place and you want to stand on soft pine needles and dirt. Maybe there are ancient rocks nearby that feel good underneath your feet. Maybe you live in the city and you have a favorite patch of grass in a nearby park. No matter your preference, you can ground anywhere.

Stand with your bare feet connecting directly to the earth. Begin by straightening your shoulders, closing your eyes, and taking a few very deep, very intentional breaths. My favorite is breathing in for a count of three, holding for a count of three, and breathing out for a count of three.

As you are breathing and your feet are on the ground, visualize the network of the earth connecting into the bottoms of your feet. I like to visualize networks of tree roots as if they were brain synapses, lighting up and connecting with my feet. Your network may look totally different, which is perfectly fine.

Once you are connected into this network, the electromagnetic fields of the earth and your body do the work. They are automatically taking the excess energy of your mind, the anxiety and overwhelm, and giving you the support of the earth. You can visualize your energy moving downward into the earth while the earth feeds you life-supporting energy. As you breathe, focus on the gratitude you feel for being with the earth and how beautiful the earth really is. Stay in this place for as long as you would like to. When you feel complete, simply come out of it, thank the earth, and continue with your ritual or your day.

If you aren't the type to feel energy or see strong visuals, that's okay too. Just make sure you're taking enough time to allow yourself to intentionally hang out with the earth. You can also do this exercise with shoes on or indoors, especially for those of us in winter climates, but any opportunity to connect your skin to the earth makes a big difference.

GRAVEYARD GROUNDING FOR ANXIETY AND MIGRAINES

This exercise is especially for instances when you can feel the excess energy in your head that may be causing anxiety or migraines. I've used this exercise in periods of intense emotional processing when I was often getting migraines.

Find a graveyard or cemetery, preferably an older one. Do this during the day.

Find a tree in that graveyard that calls to you. The older, the better. Big oak trees are always an excellent choice.

Sit at the base of the tree, facing north if possible. Push your back so it's against the tree, sit with your knees up so your bare feet are in contact with the ground, and place your hands either on the ground or at the base of the tree. You are making as much contact as you can with the tree and the ground. Sometimes, I will even turn my face so my cheek is touching the tree.

In this position, visualize the tree pulling the anxious and painful energy out of your body. It's pulling it from all angles. It's pulling from your feet, from your hands, from your back, and from your head. It's pulling the energy you don't need and it's feeding it to the earth. Breathe normally or use the 3-3-3 breath (breathe in for 3 seconds, hold for 3 seconds, and exhale for 3 seconds) and relax into it. Keep this going for at least fifteen minutes, but don't stop until you noticeably start to feel better. It will take different amounts of time with different pains.

The reason this is so powerful in a graveyard is because of the energetic cycles taking place. This is a place where the earth is feeding on the things we've left behind after our passing. This is a place where we offer our excess to the earth to be reused and reborn. The earth loves to feed on the energy we don't need anymore, especially when we give it consciously, as an offering. It also deeply connects us to both the ancestors of the land and our own ancestors, which makes any intentional energy work we do even stronger.

HEAVEN AND EARTH
GROUNDING FOR BALANCE

This grounding exercise takes a little more intentional focus and is good for when you're feeling especially ungrounded or anxious or when you're about to perform a big ritual.

You can do this exercise anywhere, whether you're outside or not. Make sure both feet, shoes off, are securely rooted to the ground or floor.

Turn your attention to the earth beneath your feet and bring awareness to your pelvis area/root chakra. Your root chakra is where your body connects into the earth energy and feeds your safety. Close your eyes and visualize a vibrant and strong tube of red light coming up from the center of the earth. This red tube of light is pure earth energy and is so powerful that it can instantly help ground you. Visualize the red tube of light connecting into your root chakra and rising up into your body.

Then, visualize a tube of divine white light coming down from the heavens. Visualize that light meeting the top of your head, your crown chakra, and going down into your body. With the red light at your root and the white light at your crown, you are perfectly balanced with the earth and the heavens.

Now, bring your attention to your heart area. Here, you'll visualize the red light and the white light meeting, turning a beautiful soft pink. This soft pink light feeds your heart and your compassion.

Do this visualization for however long you would like. You may find that even one or two minutes of it has a strong effect.

Intention

Setting intention is simply the act of deciding on your desires and stating them clearly, whether you do so by writing them down, speaking them out loud, or closely holding them in your mind. Before doing any in-depth rituals or spells, you need to know the purpose of those rituals and spells. Your intention is the anchor of your ritual and the determining factor of whether it is effective. The more clarity you can get with your intention, the better. That specificity informs your ritual, especially if you're crafting your own. Knowing exactly what your intention is will help you choose ingredients and practices that will be more meaningful and more powerful for you.

As important as having a specific intention for your spellwork is, you can still practice magick even if you don't have one. This is especially relevant if you're struggling with your mental health and don't feel like you can create a specific goal. Maybe your mind is too cluttered and you don't feel you have the mental space to set a solid intention, or maybe you don't have the juice to bring about results. That's okay, too.

I like to think that there are two approaches to magick: the magick of doing (setting specific intentions to bring about results) and the magick of knowing (practicing without a specific end goal, but with knowledge and understanding in mind). If you're using the magick of knowing, then your intention may switch from an unknown specific thing to simply the intention of learning more about yourself and the elements. By consciously deciding to interact with the elements without a clear goal in mind other than understanding, you are still working on your relationships to those elements, which builds trust and strength in your magickal practice and helps you to see your world a little differently. This approach can often deepen your understanding of yourself and how you relate to your moods, which will fuel and inform your later rituals. Sometimes, by simply playing with the wind or intently watching a fire, the elements will whisper to you what you need. And sometimes, what you need is to simply exist in those elemental currents.

This book has spells and rituals for both the magick of knowing and the magick of doing since they are the yin and yang, the receiving and creating. Employing both is necessary to be a well-rounded mood witch.

Writing Your Intentions

Take some time to write down your specific intentions before doing ritual work, especially if you're creating your ritual. In this book, each of the spells has its own built-in intention, but to make the spell more personal and specific, it's still important to be clear with that intention in your own words.

Write your intentions in one to two sentences. Most importantly, use present tense and phrase each intention as if you are already receiving what you desire. This means that you won't use phrases like "I want" or "I wish" or "I will." Instead, you'll use phrases like "I am" and "I have." This is incredibly important because for the magick to work, you need to feel the energy of your result *while* you do your ritual. For example, instead of an intention of "I wish I would stop getting panic attacks at family gatherings. I don't want to be such a mess with family," you would phrase it as "I am no longer getting panic attacks at family gatherings. I am calm and confident and every family gathering becomes easier." You'll notice that the energy of the latter statement feels much different than the former—the result already feels closer.

Also, keep in mind that while it's important to match your intentions to your desires, you also want to be realistic and realize there's a nuance in your language. In the example I gave, notice how I didn't use a phrase like "And I will never feel anxious with family again." That's because if you're struggling with panic attacks in the first place, never feeling anxious is not a realistic or fair goal for yourself. I used "And every family gathering becomes easier" because it leaves room for more and more improvement while not locking you into an unattainable goal.

Writing intentions is an art and a skill, so it takes practice. Take your intentions into ritual with you, hold them close in your mind, and speak them out loud when the time is right. The following spells and rituals will help you find clarity and how and when to do that.

Why Intention Matters

Approaching your relationship with intention is especially important if you struggle with mental imbalance or mental illness. We live in a world where we are constantly bombarded by people trying to tell us what we *should* be striving for and what our intentions *should* be. This is a problem for everyone, but it's especially problematic for those of us who have entirely different lived experiences because of our mental health difficulties. Your version of a healthy intention or goal may be completely different from what the world thinks it should be. This is especially the case with productivity and work output goals. Those struggling with their mental health will never be able to meet the ceaseless demands of the productivity machine, and the longer you stand in that stream, the more it pulls pieces of you away. Societal expectation overwhelms you with everything you should be, which scatters the energy of what you actually are. Creating a unique and individual relationship with your intention helps to eliminate that codependence and panic you feel with expectation and pulls your energy back in where it belongs so you can use it in a more balanced and empowering way.

Setting your intention for your mood magick is also an opportunity to show your respect for the magickal process. In the same way you seek balance for your mental wellness, the universe must hold a balance within the energies we work with. The First Law of Thermodynamics applies to magick in this way: energy can be changed from one form to another, but it cannot be created or destroyed. This means that if you do a ritual to eliminate your anxiety or depression, that energy cannot be eliminated, but you can take that energy and transmute it so it changes for the better and so you can use it in another way. Your grounding exercises are a clear example of this. Even though you feel like you're getting rid of your excess negative energy, what you're actually doing is feeding it to the earth. The earth uses that energy and transmutes it into fuel. You are redirecting your energy so it can be recycled, but you didn't destroy it.

Creating this distinction in your mind before you start practicing mood magick is important because, without this understanding, the human mind tends to separate moods into good and bad and subsequently wants to eliminate the bad and create the good. That kind of binary thinking works against the laws of nature, which will make your rituals and spells less effective and potentially more harmful to your mental state in the long term. While our aim is to improve our emotional and mental landscapes, we must approach each aspect with love and compassion, not hatred. Curious fluidity will always yield better magickal results than rigid binary beliefs because curious fluidity leaves room for more information, more understanding, and more wisdom.

Whichever way you decide to interact with your intention, remember that your actions after the ritual or spell matter. If you believe that your spell has power (which it does), then you must also believe that your actions have power too. This means that if you cast a spell to help ease your anxiety and then walk away and engage in a round of social media and news-binging that you know gives you anxiety, you may be contradicting your spell, thereby weakening the connection that your spell has to you. While you can't babysit the energy that you cast out into the universe for your ritual or spell, you can certainly keep your connection to your spell as clean as you can so its power can fully come back to you. In every moment, you have the opportunity to either affirm or deny your intention.

The practices of grounding and setting your intention can be rituals in and of themselves. That's how powerful and important they are. Even if you are only beginning to understand the relationship between your mental health and the elements, connecting to the earth through grounding and setting your intention to improve your peace and stability will undoubtedly begin to change your experience of yourself and the world.

CHAPTER 2

Your Personal Connection to the Elements

Even though we can all learn the universal symbols and meanings of the elements, your personal experiences with them make for a stronger magickal practice. In the same way that one size doesn't fit all when it comes to your mental wellness routine, the same goes for your elemental rituals. We all respond a little differently to life, stressors, triggers, and joy; leaning into those differences is much more effective than trying to approach all things from one point of view. Your unique point of view, your unique emotions, and your unique lived experiences are what will give your magick that extra oomph. The secret ingredient in magick is *you*, raw and unfiltered.

The best way to lean into your individual magick is by becoming aware of your mental landscapes. I use the term *mental landscape* because I want you to begin associating what happens in your mind with what happens in nature. There's an entire world, completely unique to you and your experience of life, inside of your head. It changes as you change. It reacts as you react. When the world gets to you and makes you feel unstable, the ground of your mental landscape shakes and becomes unstable. When you experience mood swings, anxiety, or depression, your mental landscape changes in response. Your emotions could be considered the weather of your mental landscape. Some of your emotions may have no lasting effect on your landscape, like a breeze that passes through. Other emotions may absolutely devastate your landscape, like a raging flood that submerges your entire internal earth.

In the same way that what you do and experience in the external world can change your internal mental landscape, what you do and experience in your mental landscape can change your external world. As within, so without. You have the power to adjust what happens in your mental landscape, even when you feel powerless.

The following exercises will help you see your individual magick as it relates to each element. I'll be using what I'm calling *preexisting positive* associations and *preexisting negative* associations. The purpose of breaking it down like this is to grasp how your mind organizes your emotions and how those emotions naturally relate to the elements of nature. We need to know the connections you are already making to the elements and how they link to your mental state. This tells us both how to most easily tap into your magick and how to avoid self-sabotage in your mental health practice. I previously emphasized the need to transcend the binary labels of positive and negative and good and bad when it comes to your moods; by tapping into these preexisting associations, you'll know exactly where to bring your self-compassion and kindness to embrace the entirety of your experience rather than continue splitting them apart. You'll know exactly where to go when you need to create more peace, and you'll know exactly where to go when you are addressing struggle. This doesn't mean that you won't create new associations or that they won't change as your mental awareness and experience changes, but the more emotional connection there is to your spellwork, the more potent it will be, so I like to start where there's emotion for you now. When you embrace your preexisting positive and preexisting negative associations, you'll be able to make elemental changes in your mental landscape so you can begin to influence your outer world by understanding and working with your inner world.

Your Relationship with Earth

THE PREEXISTING
POSITIVE

Think back to a time when you felt truly grounded, stable, and connected. When you felt safe in your body. It could be one single moment. It could be a longer period of time. Take out your journal and write down all the things you see and feel. Include images, sounds, colors, and feelings. They could be actual snapshots of the reality you experienced in that time or they could be the metaphorical imagery that pops into your head when you think of it. Nothing is off-limits.

Next, think about the element of earth. Close your eyes and sink into it. For now, think only about the positive images you associate with earth. Do you see a forest you visited and fell in love with on a vacation? Is it feeling dirt underneath your feet? A long hike on a clear day? Sitting in the grass under a tree whose leaves are orange and floating down to you? Let yourself experience the parts and images of earth that you love and write them down in your journal.

Once you've done that, look at both entries. What you're looking for is any overlap. This is where you'll find your sweet spots; this is where your predisposition for earth element magick is already strong. Is there imagery you pictured for the first experience that reflects the positive imagery you felt when you thought about earth? Maybe you felt truly grounded when you were kayaking on a mountain lake, and then you pictured a mountain range covered in trees when you thought of earth. This tells you that mountains and mountain imagery will be especially effective for you when balancing and stabilizing your mental health. Maybe you felt particularly grounded when you were getting a hot stone massage, and then you saw imagery of lying on a stone beach in the sun. This tells you that stones, especially warm stones touching your skin, will be a powerful key to your stability.

Not only are these actual physical things you can do for your mental stability, but they can also be made into magickal symbols. When doing a ritual for more stability, you know you can do the ritual outside in the sunshine with stones on your skin because you know that your association and intention will be naturally strong. Or, you can move a small stone over a candle flame to represent the same thing.

Make a list of two to five overlapping earth elemental images from your journal entries, starting with the most powerful. You can always keep this list in your back pocket, ready to automatically strengthen your earth magick.

THE PREEXISTING
NEGATIVE

Think back to a time when you felt ungrounded and unstable. When you felt depressed, trapped, or unsafe. It could be one moment or it could be a period of time. Allow yourself to sink into that experience and journal what comes up. Write down images, colors, sounds, and feelings—anything that feels relevant. You could write things you saw, metaphorical imagery, or a combination of both. Write it freely.

Next, I want you to think about the element of earth and any negative associations you have with it. Do you see a landslide destroying homes? Do you see a dark cave where you are alone? Allow yourself to write down whatever negative associations you're having with earth.

Now, it's time to look at both entries again. Do you see any overlap between your experience of feeling trapped and ungrounded and your negative associations with earth? Maybe you experienced trauma in a dark room and then saw negative earth as being underground with no windows or light. Maybe you felt depressed when you were overwhelmed by your emotions and felt stuck at the same time, and then you associated negative earth with a muddy bog that could pull you under.

Make a list of two to five connections, starting with the strongest. Knowing these connections will tell you what not to use when doing positive earth spellwork. It's a reminder of your triggers, which can be very useful if you're going through a period when avoiding your triggers is important. It's also necessary imagery if you're going to be doing emotional shadow work or working deeply with your mental imbalances. You can use your negative earth imagery to submerge into your wounds and work with them there.

Earth Symbols and Ingredients

Take note of anything you have felt naturally drawn to. These will be points of strength for you, especially powerful in your rituals.

Direction: north

Images in nature: mountains, forests, caves, cliffs, deserts, natural stone formations, mud

Colors: black, brown, red, green

Astrological signs: Taurus, Virgo, Capricorn

Raw materials: bones, wood, stones, salts, dirt collected from specific places

Metal: copper, iron

Stones: all stones have earth energy, but specifically black tourmaline, bloodstone, hematite, smoky quartz, petrified wood, red jasper, lava stone (also good for fire magick), river stones (also good for water magick)

Herbs and oils: sandalwood, pine, frankincense, cedarwood, vetiver, vanilla, rosemary

Animals: goats, bulls, forest animals (especially bears, deer, raccoons, etc.)

Your Relationship with Water

THE PREEXISTING POSITIVE

Think back to a time when you felt truly connected to your emotions and your intuition. When you felt you could easily flow and dance and love your feelings. It could be one single moment. It could be a longer period of time. Take out your journal and write down all the things you see and feel. Include images, sounds, colors, and feelings. They could be actual snapshots of the reality you experienced in that time or they could be the metaphorical imagery that pops into your head when you think of it. Nothing is off-limits.

Next, think about the element of water. Close your eyes and sink into it. Think only about the positive images you associate with water. Do you see a still lake surrounded by trees and mountains? Is it feeling a cold flowing stream on your feet? Do you see a moody sea with waves crashing against the rocks? A gentle autumn rain? Let yourself experience the parts and images of water that you love and write them down in your journal.

Once you've done that, look at both entries. What you're looking for is any overlap. This is where you'll find your sweet spots; this is where your predisposition for water magick is already strong. Is there imagery you pictured for the first experience that reflects the positive imagery you felt when you thought about water? Maybe you felt truly in touch with your emotions when you thought about a trip you took to the Maine coast, and then pictured waves against dark rocks when you thought of water. That tells you that rocky coastlines and waves will be especially effective for you for emotional healing. Maybe you felt particularly peaceful when you once went swimming at night under the moon, and then you pictured still, reflective waters when you thought of the water element. This tells you that using moonlight and calm water will be extra powerful for your peace and soothing, and also that water immersion is good for you.

Not only are these actual physical things you can do for your emotional healing but they also can be made into magickal symbols. When doing a ritual for more peace, you know you can do the ritual outside by the water because you know that your association and intention will be naturally strong. Or, you can have a small dish of water in front of you to represent the same thing.

Make a list of two to five overlapping water elemental images from your journal entries, starting with the most powerful. You can always keep this list in your back pocket, ready to automatically strengthen your water magick.

THE PREEXISTING
NEGATIVE

Think back to a time when you felt truly overwhelmed by your emotions. When you felt weepy or unable to discern what to do next. When you felt like you were drowning. It could be one moment or it could be a period of time. Allow yourself to sink into that experience and journal what comes up. Write down images, colors, sound, feelings—anything that feels relevant. You could write things you saw or it could be metaphorical imagery coming up or a combination or both. Write it freely.

Next, think about the element of water and any negative associations you have with it. Do you see a tsunami destroying coastal cities? Maybe a flood taking over your town? Drowning? Allow yourself to write down whatever negative associations you're having with water.

Now, it's time to look at both entries again. Do you see any overlap between your experience of feeling emotionally overwhelmed and your negative associations with water? Maybe you had depression during a very rainy season and now have negative associations with rain and the color gray. Maybe you felt like you were drowning in tears when you experienced significant loss or grief and now you have a strong visual tie to being underwater.

Make a list of two to five water element connections, starting with the strongest. Knowing these connections will tell you what not to use when doing positive water spellwork. It's a reminder of your triggers, which can be very useful if you're going through a period when avoiding your triggers is important. It's also necessary imagery you need to know if you're going to be doing emotional shadow work or working deeply with your mental imbalances. You can use your negative water imagery to submerge into your wounds and work with them there.

Water Symbols and Ingredients

Direction: west

Images in nature: oceans, rivers, lakes, waves, seashells, rain, moon

Colors: blue, teal, gray, silver, turquoise

Astrological signs: Pisces, Cancer, Scorpio

Raw materials: water collected from anywhere, sand, shells, sea creature fossils, seaweed, sea salt

Metal: silver

Stones: moonstone, celestite, kyanite, lapis lazuli, selenite, river rock

Herbs and oils: chamomile, rose, Irish moss, citrus, kelp

Animals: whales, dolphins, seals, mermaids, fish

Your Relationship with Fire

THE PREEXISTING
POSITIVE

Think back to a time when you felt truly passionate and alive. When you felt you could easily create what you wanted. When you felt sensual and connected to yourself and your passion, whether that passion was for a creative project, romantic partner, or personal experience. It could be one single moment. It could be a longer period of time. Take out your journal and write down all the things you see and feel. Include images, sounds, colors, and feelings. They could be actual snapshots of the reality you experienced in that time or they could be the metaphorical imagery that pops into your head when you think of it. Nothing is off-limits.

Next, think about the element of fire. Close your eyes and sink into it. Think about the positive images you associate with fire. Do you see a roaring bonfire in the woods? A perfect sunny day? Maybe a room filled with candlelight? Let yourself experience the parts and images of fire that you love and write them down in your journal.

Once you've done that, look at both entries. What you're looking for is any overlap. This is where you'll find your sweet spots; this is where your predisposition for fire elemental magick is already strong. Is there imagery you pictured for the first experience that reflects the positive imagery you felt when you thought about fire? Maybe you felt truly alive when you first made love to your partner in a candlelit room, then pictured a lot of candles for fire. That tells you that candlelight is a quick and powerful tool to connect you to your passion and sensuality. Maybe you feel creative when you do morning walks in the sunshine, and then you pictured a sunny day when you thought about your positive associations for fire. That tells you not only that the sun is a key component of your fire magick but also that movement is.

Not only are these actual physical things you can do for your passion and creativity but they also can be made into magickal symbols. When doing a ritual for more passion, you know you can do the ritual inside with candles because you know that your association and intention will be naturally strong. Or, you can have a single candle represent any of your fire associations.

Make a list of two to five overlapping fire elemental images from your journal entries, starting with the most powerful. You can always keep this list in your back pocket, ready to automatically strengthen your fire magick.

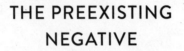

THE PREEXISTING
NEGATIVE

Think back to a time when you felt truly angry or out of control. When you felt amped up and ungrounded. It could be one moment or it could be a period of time. Allow yourself to sink into that experience and journal what comes up. Write down images, colors, sounds, and feelings. You could write things you saw, metaphorical imagery, or a combination of both. Write it freely.

Next, think about the element of fire and any negative associations you have with it. Do you see a wildfire burning up ancient forests? Maybe you see yourself as a witch being burned at the stake. Write down whatever negative associations you're having with fire.

Now, it's time to look at both entries again. Do you see any overlap between your experience of feeling angry and out of control and your negative associations with fire? Maybe you felt like everything was burning when your life felt out of control, and then you pictured a wildfire in your negative associations, or you pictured yourself on fire. This tells you that you'll need to have your fire safely contained in all your rituals to avoid triggers.

Make a list of two to five connections, starting with the strongest. Knowing these connections will tell you what not to use when doing positive fire spellwork. It's a reminder of your triggers, which can be very useful if you're going through a period when avoiding your triggers is important. It's also necessary imagery you need to know if you're going to be doing emotional shadow work or working deeply with your mental imbalances. You can use your negative fire imagery to submerge into your wounds and work with them there.

Fire Symbols and Ingredients

Direction: south

Images in nature: wildfires, volcanoes, bonfires, embers, candle flames, lightning, sun

Colors: red, orange, amber, yellow

Astrological signs: Aries, Leo, Sagittarius

Raw materials: ash, candle wax, flame, coals, cinnamon, cayenne

Metal: gold

Stones: citrine, pyrite, carnelian, lava stone, topaz

Herbs and oils: black pepper, cinnamon, clove, ginger, juniper, rosemary, citrus

Animals: lions, salamanders, foxes, lizards, dragons, phoenixes, hot climate animals like giraffes and zebras

Your Relationship with Air

THE PREEXISTING POSITIVE

Think back to a time when you felt really inspired, when you felt like you could easily move forward in life with clarity. It could be one single moment. It could be a longer period of time. Take out your journal and write down all the things you see and feel. Include images, sounds, colors, and feelings. They could be actual snapshots of the reality you experienced in that time or they could be the metaphorical imagery that pops into your head when you think of it. Nothing is off-limits.

Next, think about the element of air. Close your eyes and sink into it. Think about the positive images you associate with air. Do you see a gentle summer breeze in the trees? A flurry of leaves in an autumn gust? An intense wave storm that captivates you? A flock of birds flying? Let yourself experience the parts and images of air that you love and write them down in your journal.

Once you've done that, look at both entries. What you're looking for is any overlap. This is where you'll find your sweet spots; this is where your predisposition for air element magick is already strong. Is there imagery you pictured for the first experience that reflects the positive imagery you felt when you thought about air? Maybe you felt truly inspired when you had a sudden rush of new ideas and then pictured swirling leaves in your positive imagery. This tells you that swirls and rushes will be powerful air imagery for you to use when invoking inspiration. Maybe you felt really in touch with your ideas in a time period when you took things slow and gentle, and then imagined a slight breeze in your positive air imagery. This tells you that your air magick will be better off with gentler manifestations instead of large gusts.

Not only are these actual physical things you can do for your mental wellness but they also can be made into magickal symbols. When doing a ritual for more inspiration, you know you can do the ritual outside on a gusty day because you have that association already. You can also use incense smoke and even your breath to represent your sweet spot with air.

Make a list of two to five overlapping air elemental images from your journal entries, starting with the most powerful. You can always keep this list in your back pocket, ready to automatically strengthen your air magick.

THE PREEXISTING NEGATIVE

Think back to a time when you felt really disconnected and distracted. When you felt like your body was miles away and you couldn't focus on anything. It could be one moment or it could be a period of time. Allow yourself to sink into that experience and journal what comes up. Write down images, colors, sounds, and feelings. You could write things you saw, metaphorical imagery, or a combination of both. Write it freely.

Next, think about the element of air and any negative associations you have with it. Do you see a tornado coming through? Do you see a sudden strong gust that comes out of nowhere, rustling up and changing things you don't want changed? Allow yourself to write down whatever negative associations you're having with air.

Now, it's time to look at both entries again. Do you see any overlap between your experience of feeling distracted and unfocused and your negative associations with air? Maybe you felt like all your progress was easily swept away, and then you pictured that sudden gust. Maybe what you felt was just the fear of suddenly losing yourself in your lack of focus, and then you imagined a tornado ripping you up.

Make a list of two to five connections, starting with the strongest. Knowing these connections will tell you what not to use when doing positive air spellwork. It's a reminder of your triggers, which can be very useful if you're going through a period when avoiding your triggers is important. It's also necessary imagery you need to know if you're going to be doing emotional shadow work or working deeply with your mental imbalances. You can use your negative air imagery to submerge into your wounds and work with them there.

Air Symbols and Ingredients

Direction: east

Images in nature: breeze, tornadoes, storms, waves, leaves, feathers, flowers, smoke

Colors: white, blue, green, yellow

Astrological signs: Gemini, Libra, Aquarius

Raw materials: feathers, ash, dust, smoke

Metal: silver or gold

Stones: amethyst, diamond, opal, moldavite, fluorite, quartz

Herbs and oils: spearmint, ylang-ylang, neroli, tea tree, jasmine

Animals: all birds, dragonflies (also a water creature)

When taking stock of your elemental associations, make sure to look for themes in your life you may not realize are playing out. Recurring dreams are one great place to look. Our dreams often contain very primal and elemental symbolism, offering us some of the most potent keys to our magick. They also tend to give you very literal assistance, like when you dream of a magickal object that you need to use for your next ritual.

Another unexpected place to look is in your hobbies and your career. What are your natural skills? If you work with emotions a lot, you have a lot of water in you. Wanderlust and the urge to float around searching for adventure can indicate a strong drive for air magick. If you invoke a lot of passion in your life, fire may be your primary elemental expression. Earth might be your natural position if you tend to be the stable and responsible one among your family and friends. Your astrological chart will also offer a ton of insight into your relationship to the elements. Even the place you grew up will help determine your elemental associations. Your relationship to your magick is your own, so you will often find clues scattered about for you to pick up along the way.

Knowing your preexisting associations with the elements will help you see, shape, and transform your inner mental landscapes. Being aware of your power to make those shifts will help you more easily create stability, peace, and healing in your mental health practice.

CHAPTER 3

Easy Elemental Spells

The world of elemental magick can seem intimidating at first, but it can be made simple and easy to integrate into your daily life and mental wellness routine. All you need is your imagination, your intentions, and some guidelines and rituals to help you direct them.

For many who aren't familiar with witchcraft, the idea of beginning a practice can make them feel a bit silly or self-conscious. That self-consciousness can even prevent people from truly giving it a go. Given that most people have only seen witchcraft done dramatically in movies, TV shows, and books like *The Craft, Charmed, Practical Magic, A Discovery of Witches*, etc., it's completely understandable to feel a little hesitant or shy. If that's you, that's totally okay, and may even work to your advantage.

Since magick is simply metaphor made real, those dramatic visuals and elemental interactions you see in movies can be incredibly powerful. You may have already used this kind of magick without realizing. Have you ever listened to your favorite songs and imagined yourself as the star in the music video, wearing dramatic costumes, and acting out the lyrics in specific places? Have you ever been so sucked into a movie in the moment where everything builds, the music swells, the wind kicks up, and then a crash of emotion completes it? This is mood magick. You can carry this into your practice, even if you're unsure of what you're doing. It's supposed to be fun, so don't be afraid to pretend you're in a music video or movie at first. It's very similar to a guided meditation or visualization, and you may find that specific images make you feel tuned into your power more than others.

I'm a lover of moody music, so I find that using specific songs or playlists really helps me create and slip into a specific mood magick ritual and my images of my power. If you're more stimulated by visual art, use art pieces that evoke the emotions you're working with. You can also bring your imagination to life with what you wear. I have often pictured myself in a flowing gauzy dress, high atop the cliffs in Ireland, overlooking the sea as the wind whips my hair around and the clouds darken. Because of this, I enjoy wearing flowing dresses during air and water rituals outside. I'll even swim in dresses for that sensual mood when I'm connecting with the water element.

For fire and earth, I often picture myself in a dark room full of candles, fur rugs on the floor, reds and golds everywhere, and my body adorned in black lace. So, when I go to practice many of my indoor fire and earth rituals, that's exactly how you find me: surrounded by candles, wearing black lace, with a faux fur rug beneath me, connecting into the sensuality I felt in my imagination. Making it real for myself. Even if my ritual doesn't work and has absolutely no effect on the real world, even if I just consider it "play," I still have a visceral and sensual experience I fully enjoy and it shifts my mood. If that's how you need to approach it at first, go ahead! Even with this attitude, however, your ritual will still create change. If you willingly engage your imagination in this process, it will have an effect.

Embracing your drama and your imagination accentuates and builds your unique power and the power of your rituals and spells. Maybe in your imagination, you see yourself in a bright room full of prisms and rainbows. To make it real, you can hang prisms in your windows (or use prism window clings) and do your ritual during the time of day that room receives the most light. Maybe you see yourself submerged in hot springs under the moon. To make it real, you could take a hot bath in only the light of the moon and perform your ritual or spell while being submerged in the water. Your options are limitless.

Don't be afraid to embrace your drama and bring it into all your rituals. Your mood magick isn't the same without it.

In this chapter, you'll find easy elemental spells and rituals you can do to set up your practice, engage your imagination and your drama, and build your magickal muscles. You'll also learn how to work with the preexisting positive and preexisting negative associations of the elements you explored from the previous chapter.

Create an Altar

Creating an altar is a simple way to bring in all the elements and it's a good foundational practice to build the rest of your mood magick on. You simply need to choose a space that will specifically be used only as your altar. This could be on a small table, bookshelf, fireplace mantel, or even a rug in the corner of a room. On your altar, you need at least one physical object to represent each element. These objects can be unique to you, but there are some really easy choices to get you started. For earth, you can use stones and crystals. For air, incense or feathers. For fire, go for candles. For water, you can use an actual dish of water or use an object that represents water, like a seashell. You can also add in any other sacred objects to you, whether they're family photos, figurines, ritual tools, rosaries or malas, tarot cards, etc. You'll often find my altar adorned with gifts I find from nature—agates, sea glass, tree bark, animal bones, snakeskin. I also like to rotate some of my family items or ritual tools throughout the year, depending on what I'm focusing on.

Having your altar can constantly remind you of the elements and your magickal practice. It's the best place to sit and meditate or pray, and ideally, you'll do a lot of your rituals in the same space as your altar.

Try to engage with your altar for at least a moment every day. Light a candle. Touch your precious items. Say a small prayer or say hello to your ancestors. All these things keep your altar activated.

ELEMENTAL OPENING RITUAL

This is an easy ritual to create a protected circle for your magick and to bring all four elements into that circle. If you only have time for one elemental ritual, this is the one I would recommend. Do this before you do any of your other ritual work since it activates your space, creates a protective ring around you, and only takes a couple of minutes.

Stand in the middle of the room, close your eyes, and focus on your breathing. Make sure you feel grounded to the earth. Hold both palms out in front of you, like you're motioning "stop" to someone in front of you. Opening your eyes, slowly turn clockwise with your palms out. Visualize a huge wall of bright beautiful white light or fire that your own hands are creating with each exhale, as if exhaling is what releases the light from your hands. The further you turn, the more of the beautiful light wall you build, until you've made a full circle and your entire space is protected by that white light. This has activated your magick circle.

Stand with palms open at your sides.

Facing north, say:

> I call upon the watchtower of the north and the element of earth.
> May earth secure me and ground me in my sacred circle.

Visualize your positive earth associations from chapter 2. I like to do this for each element for an entire minute or two until I can feel the energy tingling in my body.

Turning clockwise to face east, say:

> I call upon the watchtower of the east and the element of air. May
> air move me and inspire me in my sacred circle.

Visualize your positive air associations.

Turning clockwise to face south, say:

> I call upon the watchtower of the south and the element of fire. May fire surround my circle and burn up anything that is not for my highest good.

Visualize your positive fire associations.

Turning clockwise to face west, say:

> I call upon the watchtower of the west and the element of water. May water soothe me and heal me in my circle.

Visualize your positive water associations.

Turning clockwise to face north again, say:

> I call upon the divine spirit (feel free to insert your own language here that fits with your preferred traditions) to weave together the four elements within my mind, body, and within this circle. So be it.

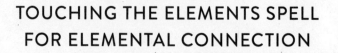

TOUCHING THE ELEMENTS SPELL FOR ELEMENTAL CONNECTION

This is a short and easy spell to connect the metaphor of the elements to the actual elements themselves. By doing this ritual, you'll begin to get clarity on what kind of mood magick will be best for you. Do this spell as many times as you would like.

What you need:

- stone of any kind
- bowl of water
- bit of salt or ash
- candle

Pick up your stone and while holding it in your hands, say:

Earth. My body.

Place the stone into the bowl of water, letting the tips of your fingers touch the water.

Say, *Water. My emotions.*

Pinch a bit of the salt or ash into your hand, then lightly blow it into the bowl of water.

Say, *Air. My mind.*

Then, pass your hand over the candle flame, close enough to feel the warmth.

Say, *Fire. My passion.*

Hold your arms out, palms up, and say:

The four create the whole.

As my spirit stands center,

I am connected to each,

and my magick becomes clear.

Put your hands in prayer position over your heart.

So be it.

Elemental Rituals for the Positive and Negative

These rituals are incredibly important for working with and defining your elemental strengths and weaknesses. They are the foundation for transformation. You'll need to refer back to your preexisting positive and preexisting negative associations from chapter 2, as you'll be heavily using that imagery here. You will also need physical objects to represent your positive associations of the elements. Whatever those objects are, they need to feel right. Don't pick something just because you think it's logical. Your objects have to feel good in your hands and they have to make you think of your positive associations with the elements. With consistent use, you'll start to feel how these images and objects reflect your emotions and vice versa, giving you another tool in understanding the way your mental health operates and a simple but effective way to mold it in an empowering way.

RITUAL FOR POSITIVE EARTH

To increase stability and safety and decrease anxiety, trauma, and mania.

This is a very simple ritual to incorporate more earth into your life. All you're really doing is taking the grounding exercises and including your representations of positive earth into it.

For this ritual, you will need a physical representation of your positive earth elemental images from your journal entries. Something you can hold in your hand. What this object is, is entirely up to you. It could be a warm stone. It could be a jar of dirt from your favorite forest you pictured. It could be a little figurine of a mountain.

Ideally, you want to be sitting outside on the actual earth, but you can do this anywhere. Hold your object in your hand and close your eyes. Begin by doing a grounding exercise. Imagine your excess energy being drained into the earth and a pure red light meeting the base of your spine to fill you with clear and vibrant earth energy. Imagine warmth coming from the object in your hand along with a sparkling, golden energy. The warmth slowly spreads throughout your entire body and the golden color interacts with the red, creating a beautiful amber color that radiates from your skin. All at once, your body is being drained of excess energy and filled with warm, grounding energy.

Slightly raise your head toward the sky and inhale. As you exhale, intentionally smile. Focus your attention on your positive images of earth—let them take over your mind and your body.

Say out loud,
> I welcome the grounding influence of the earth.
> I welcome the gentle and warming energy of earth in motion.
> I am stable and centered.
> I am both quiet and still, and also moving forward.
> I am earth.
> So be it.

RITUAL FOR NEGATIVE EARTH

To transform wounds of depression, anxiety, and trauma.

This ritual is like the previous one, but with an added focus on shifting from your negative earth images into your positive ones. This is only to be done when you are feeling safe enough to face your negative associations and experiences.

Just as before, sit on the earth, holding your earth object. First, you will visualize the things you saw when you did the negative earth journal entries. Breathe deeply as you let the pictures and feelings grow bigger and stronger. Let the colors and shapes form and let yourself feel the negative emotion you felt before. Let yourself see this entire landscape. Once this mental landscape is formed, continue to breathe deeply and notice the different elements in your picture. Allow yourself to remember the experiences that created this place. Notice how it's different from the visual of your positive earth images and your experiences with that.

As you look around, start thinking about how you can change the landscape with your imagination so it becomes your positive association. For example, maybe your negative earth is dark and muddy while your positive earth is dry with the sun hanging above you. If this is the case, imagine bringing the sun into your negative image and watching it light up the scene and dry up the mud. If your negative image is in a swamp and your positive image is on a mountain, once you dry the swamp with the sun, visualize the landscape changing and flowing so it becomes a mountain. Let your imagination run wild as it changes your negative landscape into your positive one. You are the creator here and it is through your willpower that this will happen.

Once your landscape has changed, continue with the positive earth ritual, using the grounding visualization, the warm, golden energy from the object in your hand, and the incantation.

You may have to do this multiple times, and you may find that your landscape changes often. You can continue to form your landscape in the way that you like as long as you continue using the golden energy and the incantation to close. By doing this, you are assigning symbolism to your feelings of groundedness and ungroundedness, and working with them using those symbols.

RITUAL FOR POSITIVE WATER

To increase intuition, flow, and emotional healing while decreasing trauma, depression, and apathy.

This is a very simple ritual to incorporate more water into your life.

All you need for this ritual is a physical representation of your positive water elemental images from your journal entries. Something you can hold in your hand. What this object is, is entirely up to you. It could be a seashell. It could be a jar of water from the sea. It could be a little figurine of a mermaid or a whale.

Ideally, you want to be outside near water, but you can do this anywhere. Hold your object in your hand and close your eyes. Imagine yourself surrounded by your positive images of water. Maybe you see yourself swimming in the ocean or sitting in the rain. See those images of water begin to glow and notice the color. It could be a seafoam green, a stormy blue, or a deep turquoise. Once you can see your water images glowing with this color, shift your focus to the object in your hand. That object begins to glow a light golden color and it radiates outward until that color meets the color of the water and you are surrounded by these beautiful swirling colors that move and gently rock you, comforting you.

Slightly raise your head toward the sky and inhale. As you exhale, intentionally smile. Focus your attention on your positive images of water. Let them take over your mind and your body.

Say out loud:

    I welcome the healing influence of water.

    I welcome the still depths of my intuition,

    and the rushing movement of my emotions.

    I am fluid. I am in flow.

    I am both in tune with the waves of my moods,

    and embrace grace with their changes.

    I am water.

    So be it.

RITUAL FOR NEGATIVE WATER

To transform wounds of emotional overwhelm and intense mood swings.

This ritual is like the previous one, but with an added focus on shifting from your negative water images into your positive ones. This is only to be done when you are feeling safe enough to face your negative associations and experiences.

Just as before, sit by the water, holding your water object. First, you will visualize the things you saw when you did the negative water journal entries. Breathe deeply as you let the pictures and feelings grow bigger and stronger. Let the colors and shapes form and let yourself feel the negative emotion you felt before. Let yourself see this entire landscape. Once this mental landscape is formed, continue to breathe deeply and notice the different elements in your picture. Allow yourself to remember the experiences that created this place. Notice how it's different from the visual of your positive water images and your experiences with that.

As you look around, start thinking about how you can change the landscape with your imagination so it becomes your positive association. For example, maybe your negative water is dark and chaotic, like being trapped in the waves in the dead of night, while your positive water is calm. If this is the case, imagine the moon rising above the water while the waves calm, so you can watch the reflection of the moon on the still water as everything quiets down. If your negative image is a stagnant muddy river and your positive image is a big lake surrounded by trees, imagine yourself following that river faster and faster until it leads you to the big clear lake. Let your imagination run wild as it changes your negative landscape into your positive one. You are the creator here and it is through your willpower that this will happen.

Once your landscape has changed, you will continue with the positive water ritual, using the visualization, the golden energy from the object in your hand, and the incantation.

You may have to do this multiple times, and you may find that your landscape changes often. You can continue to form your landscape in the way that you like as long as you continue using the golden energy and the incantation to close. By doing this, you are assigning symbolism to your feelings of being in flow with your emotions and being overwhelmed by them, and working with them using those symbols.

RITUAL FOR POSITIVE AIR

To increase inspiration and forward movement while decreasing depression and apathy.

This is a very simple ritual to incorporate more air into your life.

All you need for this ritual is a physical representation of your positive air elemental images from your journal entries. Something you can hold in your hand. What this object is, is entirely up to you. It could be a feather. It could be a leaf from your favorite tree. It could be a little figurine of a bird.

Ideally, you want to be outside where there's at least a little bit of a breeze, but you can do this anywhere. Hold your object in your hand and close your eyes. Imagine yourself surrounded by your positive images of air. Maybe you see yourself on a mountain as your hair whips in the wind, or maybe you imagine yourself flying. See those images of air begin to glow and notice the color. It could be a golden yellow, a light green, even a pale white. Once you can see your air images glowing with this color, shift your focus to the object in your hand. That object begins to glow a light golden color and it radiates outward until that color meets the color of the air, and you are surrounded by these beautiful moving colors that flow across your skin and gently move you.

Slightly raise your head toward the sky and inhale. As you exhale, intentionally smile. Focus your attention on your positive images of air. Let them take over your mind and your body.

Say out loud:

> I welcome the inspirational influence of air.
>
> I welcome the joyful push toward my dreams
>
> and the ever-changing movement of ideas.
>
> I am changeable. I am in my wisdom.
>
> I embrace the way I communicate with purpose,
>
> and I let the wind blow away what doesn't serve that purpose.
>
> I am air.
>
> So be it.

RITUAL FOR NEGATIVE AIR

To transform wounds of anxiety, mania, lack of focus, and ungroundedness.

This ritual is like the previous one, but with an added focus on shifting from your negative air images into your positive ones. This is only to be done when you are feeling safe enough to face your negative associations and experiences.

Just as before, sit in the breeze, holding your air object. First, you will visualize the things you saw when you did the negative air journal entries. Breathe deeply as you let the pictures and feelings grow bigger and stronger. Let the colors and shapes form. Let yourself feel the negative emotion you felt before. Let yourself see this entire landscape. Once this mental landscape is formed, continue to breathe deeply and notice the different elements in your picture. Allow yourself to remember the experiences that created this place. Notice how it's different from the visual of your positive air images and your experiences with that.

As you look around, start thinking about how you can change the land-scape with your imagination so it becomes your positive association. For example, maybe your negative air is running from a tornado while your positive air is much calmer. If this is the case, imagine the tornado disap-pearing up into the sky while the sun comes out and only a gentle breeze is left. If your negative image is that there is no air at all, like you're trapped underground, imagine air suddenly moving all around, blowing away everything that traps you, and lifting you onto your feet. Let your imagination run wild as it changes your negative landscape into your posi-tive one. You are the creator here and it is through your willpower that this will happen.

Once your landscape has changed, continue with the positive air ritual, using the visualization, the golden energy from the object in your hand, and the incantation.

You may have to do this multiple times, and you may find that your landscape changes often. You can continue to form your landscape in the way that you like as long as you continue using the golden energy and the incantation to close. By doing this, you are assigning symbolism to your feelings of being stagnant or uninspired and being inspired and moving forward, and working with them using those symbols.

RITUAL FOR POSITIVE FIRE

To increase creativity, passion, and purpose while decreasing depression and loneliness.

This is a very simple ritual to incorporate more fire into your life. You can do this outside by a bonfire or inside with candles. All you need for this ritual is a physical representation of your positive fire elemental images from your journal entries. Something you can hold in your hand. What this object is, is entirely up to you. It could be a red stone. It could be a charred piece of wood. The easiest option for this is simply holding a lit candle or having one right in front of you.

Hold your object in your hand and close your eyes. Imagine yourself surrounded by your positive images of fire. Maybe you see yourself lit in the soft glow of candles or maybe you see yourself by a bonfire in the middle of the woods. See those images of fire begin to glow and notice the color. It will likely be a red, an orange, or an amber hue. Notice how it flickers like fire. Once you can see your fire images glowing with this color, shift your focus to the object in your hand. That object begins to glow a golden color and it radiates outwards until that color meets the color of the fire, and you are surrounded by these beautiful flickering colors that light up your skin and warm your body.

Slightly raise your head toward the sky and inhale. As you exhale, intentionally smile. Focus your attention on your positive images of fire. Let them take over your mind and your body.

Say out loud:

I welcome the passionate spark of fire.

I welcome the warm loving glow of the embers in my cells

and the creative yearning in my belly.

I am bright and sensual and connected.

I embrace the passion of my body and my creativity

and I let the flames burn up all that doesn't serve love.

I am fire.

So be it.

RITUAL FOR NEGATIVE FIRE

To transform wounds of passion, creativity, depression, and anxiety.

This ritual is like the previous one, but with an added focus on shifting from your negative fire images into your positive ones. This is only to be done when you are feeling safe enough to face your negative associations and experiences.

Just as before, sit with your candle or with your fire object. First, visualize the things you saw when you did the negative fire journal entries. Breathe deeply as you let the pictures and feelings grow bigger and stronger. Let the colors and shapes form. Let yourself feel the negative emotion you felt before. Let yourself see this entire landscape. Once this mental landscape is formed, continue to breathe deeply and notice the different elements in your picture. Allow yourself to remember the experiences that created this place. Notice how it's different from the visual of your positive fire images and your experiences with that.

As you look around, start thinking about how you can change the landscape with your imagination so it becomes your positive association. For example, maybe your negative fire is a wildfire while your positive fire is a calm candle flame. If this is the case, imagine the wildfire dissipating into the air, leaving only one small candle on the forest floor instead. If your negative image is being in a house on fire and your positive image is simple sunshine, imagine that the fire can burn everything up, including yourself, and then imagine yourself rising from the ashes, reborn in a beautiful ray of sunshine. Let your imagination run wild as it changes your negative landscape into your positive one. You are the creator here and it is through your willpower that this will happen.

Once your landscape has changed, continue with the positive fire ritual, using the visualization, the golden energy from the object in your hand, and the incantation.

You may have to do this multiple times and you may find that your landscape changes often. You can continue to form your landscape in the way that you like as long as you continue using the golden energy and the incantation to close. By doing this, you are assigning symbolism to your feelings of being disconnected and connected in passion, and working with them using those symbols.

Too Little or Too Much for Elemental Balance

Since we are all made up of the elements, both physically and symbolically, we can find that having too much or too little of each element has a deep impact on us. Here are some of the common ways that too little or too much of each element manifests. Though, keep in mind that these manifestations can be unique to each person, which is why it's important for you to know your personal associations. In general, you can add more of one element to balance out too much of another, like increasing water to balance out fire and increasing earth to balance out air.

Signs and Symptoms of Too Little Earth

- feeling unfocused

- dissociation

- drifting from one thing to another

- anxiety

- disconnection or separation from roots and family

- being unable to commit or feeling indecisive

- feeling unsafe or unprotected

- dizziness/lightheadedness

Little Things You Can Do to Bring More Earth into Your Space

- have Himalayan salt lamps in multiple rooms

- carry your favorite stones in your pocket, purse, etc.

- intentionally place larger stones in corners of your home

- buy furniture that naturally showcases the wood it was made from

- use and display plenty of natural skincare products like bath salts and clay masks

- display landscape or nature photos on your walls

Signs and Symptoms of Too Much Earth

- feeling stagnant

- being unable to move forward

- feeling uninspired

- depression

- resentment or unhealthy dynamics in family and relationships

- vague aches and pain in the body

- self-sabotage from stubbornness

Little Things You Can Do to Remove Excess Earth in Your Space

- sweep the floors

- declutter your home

- smoke cleanse with herbs such as sage and cedar

- use a salt scrub in the shower

- clean dirty or dusty surfaces

- open your windows for fresh air

Signs and Symptoms of Too Little Water

- feeling out of touch with your emotions

- disconnection from God

- feeling stuck or out of flow

- coldness or strictness in relationships

- dryness and bloating in the body

- control freak habits

- overly rigid boundaries

Little Things You Can Do to Bring More Water into Your Space

- regularly use natural room and body mists

- take more showers and baths

- keep fresh flowers in vases in the home

- drink water

- drink more water

- sing and dance

- move your body more in whatever ways feel good

- have honest conversations

- allow yourself to cry

Signs and Symptoms of Too Much Water

- weeping spells

- feeling overwhelmed by your feelings

- being easily emotionally triggered

- codependence in relationships

- lack of boundaries

Little Things You Can Do to Remove Excess Water in Your Space

- check your home's faucets and pipes for leaks and fix them

- make an effort to get more sunshine or invest in a natural light lamp

- light a lot of candles

- make sure you're physically warm enough and snuggle in blankets if you're not

Signs and Symptoms of Too Little Air

- feeling stuck or stagnant

- a lack of inspiration

- excessive stubbornness

- lack of interest in your hobbies and curiosities

- feeling like everything is pointless

Little Things You Can Do to Bring More Air into Your Space

- open your windows to let the fresh air inside

- take more walks outside, especially when there's a breeze

- bring plants into your home

- spend more time watching how the leaves move in the trees around you

- learn something new, whether it's reading a new book, taking a class, or having a friend tell you about their interests

Signs and Symptoms of Too Much Air

- mania

- anxiety

- feeling ungrounded or unstable

- not being able to follow through with ideas

- a tendency to keep moving from place to place, job to job, or relationship to relationship

Little Things You Can Do to Remove Excess Air in Your Space

- take salt baths

- place grounding stones or crystals around your house

- put a fresh air filter in

- do a media (social media, TV, movies, etc.) cleanse for a few days

- take things off your to-do list and focus on resting

Signs and Symptoms of Too Little Fire

- depression

- feeling uninspired or having a lack of passion

- difficulty connecting in your relationships

- not being able to stand up for yourself or maintain your boundaries

- cold hands and feet

Little Things You Can Do to Bring More Fire into Your Space

- candles, candles, candles

- if you have a fireplace, use it

- focus on ambient lighting that makes you feel cozy and comfortable

- increase your heat with hot baths or blankets

- get more sunlight

- express yourself, in whatever way you can

- exercise and movement, including sex

Signs and Symptoms of Too Much Fire

- excess heat in the body (hot flashes, skin rashes, etc.)

- mania

- anxiety

- self-destructive habits, especially in love

- infatuation and obsession

- excess rage or anger

Little Things You Can Do to Remove Excess Fire in Your Space

- take cooling baths

- drink lots of water

- spend time meditating in the dark

- do rituals in moonlight instead of sunlight

- do creative projects that channel your anger or rage

- do high-intensity workouts

Knowing how the balance of the elements manifests inside yourself will help you figure out how to build a magickal practice to bring yourself and those elements back into balance. For example, if you are feeling manic and anxious, you know that you need more earth and water. So, you can turn to grounding rituals or water rituals to help you address it. If you're feeling stagnant and uninspired, then you know you have too much earth and you will need to balance it out in your ritual work with fire and air.

Knowing your natural predispositions to the elements also helps with knowing how you need to balance them. For example, if you know your astrological chart and it's mostly earth and fire signs, then you know you are more prone to stubbornness and you'll need water and air rituals to balance yourself out. You may also find that you're particularly sensitive to the amount of an element you have and can easily move out of balance by having too much or too little.

For me, that unbalanced element is earth. I have virtually no earth in my astrological chart and I also struggle with the instability that bipolar mood swings can cause, so it's incredibly important for me to get that extra grounding and stability. However, because stability is not a natural feeling for me, I can easily get too much earth and then end up feeling really stuck. Feeling how you shift with each element takes a lot of awareness of your mental health and emotional process, especially since those moods tend to shift a lot, particularly when the world feels so chaotic. It's like building a strong knowledge of your mental wellness triggers, but then going a step further by metaphorically applying those triggers with the elements.

All these simple spells and tools will help you shape a personal relationship with the elements, not only teaching you about yourself and how you relate to the world but also creating opportunities and insight into working with your own mental landscape, even as the demands of the world are constantly shaking it.

CHAPTER 4

Soothing Spells for Peace and Healing

Peace and healing can seem like difficult things to come by when you're struggling with your mental health. Feeling anxiety and overstimulation usually indicates that you need to add the soothing influence of water. Water is the element of emotions. It is the realm of the intuitive and the dreamy. It is fluid and naturally ebbs and flows, in the same way that our own emotions are fluid and naturally ebb and flow.

This makes water a very powerful element to work with when wanting to invite more peace and comfort into your life, especially when added to the grounding power of earth, the igniting power of fire, and the inventive power of air. We can guide the flow of water as we can guide the flow of our emotions, and we can balance that flow by weaving the other elements into the rituals as well. The spells and rituals in this chapter balance this flow, and are created especially for those who are under the influence of moods that tend to be high-strung or tightly wound, and those who struggle with anxiety, mania, and compounded trauma.

There are also moon spells to this chapter. While moon spells can fit into any of the elements and can be used for any mood when incorporated with thought and intention, I've chosen to place them within their primary element, water, for ease of use. Working with the moon is such a powerful and effective tool for witches of all levels since the moon rules intuition, emotions, and depth. The power of the moon is so strong that it affects the tides. It creates cycles of renewal and release, even in the physical body as menstruation. To disregard the moon when it comes to our mental health would be a waste of the empowering and clarifying influence that it is. Understanding the moon can change the way you approach your emotions and how you access your inner peace. Since the energy of the moon changes with each phase, I've included spells for each of the phases. For these spells, sitting under the light of the moon is ideal whenever possible. A bathtub is a good place too since the bathtub is just a giant cauldron.

Because a lot of these rituals involve the water element and supporting forces like the moon, I want to note the importance of intuition in your magickal practice. Since water is the element of intuition and emotions, the longer you work with water, the stronger your intuitive abilities become. As you practice these spells and rituals, you'll notice feelings you haven't noticed before. Feelings that slowly bring awareness to your life. Feelings that slap you in the face with sudden direction. Feelings that make you realize you know way more than you think you do.

Trust those instincts. If you have struggled with mental health issues or mental illness before, it's possible that you've been told that your feelings aren't trustworthy. This isn't true, though. You can experience emotional difficulty *and* trust yourself at the same time. A magickal practice is key in developing that trust in a way that both validates your mental health struggles and offers structure to your growing emotional awareness.

INTENTIONAL WEEPING RITUAL
FOR EMOTIONAL RELEASE

This ritual is as simple as it sounds, but its power runs deep. When we struggle with our mental health, we can often view crying spells or emotional outbursts as a negative sign, as an indication that what we feel is wrong and that we are failing. So, we try to repress those urges, which not only makes those emotions spill out at the worst times but it also forces us to hold an exhausting amount of tension in our bodies. Going against our bodies to maintain the image that we're not failing keeps us disconnected from our bodies, and because we're holding all that tension inside, it contributes to mental overstimulation. This ritual remedies that feeling of disconnection and engages our emotions and our bodies in an intentional way, giving those outbursts a sacred direction.

Do this ritual when you are feeling those crying spells, emotional outbursts, or intense mood swings coming on. The idea here is not to force yourself to experience outbursts and swings, but to give those naturally occurring urges a positive and safe space to exist. Basically, you're making the most of your intense difficult emotions and giving them a divine purpose.

The only things you need to do this are a dedicated time and space. The same space where you do your other rituals is best, but wherever you can feel cozy and safe is great. If you have the energy to, do the Elemental Opening Ritual and a grounding exercise. Turn off your phone, put on music if you'd like, and get rid of all distractions.

Greet your guides, ancestors, God, whatever and whoever you want to be there for you in this moment. Allow yourself to have your crying spell. Allow yourself to have your emotional outburst. Since this is your intention, being able to cry is welcome and needed instead of repressed and demonized. Speak out loud what you are feeling. Even if you know a negative feeling you're having isn't actually true, speak it out loud anyways. Maybe this speaking out loud sounds more like yelling, sobbing, or it may even be unintelligible. Allow each sob, each word you yell, each sound, to carry out the energy that was inside of you. Those words and sounds were holding all that tension in your body—release them. Don't censor yourself. If you're feeling hatred, express it. If you're feeling guilt or regret, express it. No one is here to judge you.

Take this intentional weeping a step further by asking God/your guides for what you need. Ask for help, out loud. We often forget to ask the Divine for help, and this simple thing can have such an impact. Continue this intentional expression of your feelings until your body settles and you feel tired and complete. You'll find that your body has released a lot of tension and that your mind has more clarity and room. It helps you get back to regular functioning sooner, and you may find that you are receiving assistance fairly quickly from the Divine.

Repeat this process as often as needed. I've done it for twenty minutes one day a week as a maintenance cry, and I've also done it for a few hours a day for four days straight during a depressive episode. There's no time limit, and each time will be unique with your shifting mental landscape. You'll notice that the way you see your crying spells will begin to shift, reinforcing the idea that even your negative or emotional outbursts are magickally and mentally useful and healthy.

Make sure to include aftercare. Hydration is especially important. Eat foods that make you feel grounded like root vegetables, meat, or chocolate. Sleep. Be gentle with yourself as much as you can when you're still feeling raw or emotionally hungover.

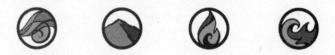

THE JAR RITUAL FOR FOCUSING AND RELEASING FEELINGS

This ritual directs your feelings to one physical point—a jar—and allows you to release them from your body so you can feel a little clearer and more at ease. This practice requires visualization and using your imagination, so if that's difficult, just start by practicing a few minutes at a time. Do this when you're feeling anxious or depressed, or when you feel like you are carrying too many negative emotions and swinging moods inside your body. All you need is a small jar that has some type of lid.

Sit with your jar in front of you, lid off. Take deep cleansing breaths and close your eyes. Allow yourself to feel your feelings of anxiety, depression, or anger without censoring yourself. Imagine those feelings as little bits of energy that actually leave your body. For me, I usually see them as little sparkles, like little brain synapses firing. They're often red or blue for me, but yours may look entirely different. Imagine those feelings, those little bits of energy, going straight into the jar in front of you. You may want to hold your jar in your hands or rest it up against your root chakra or maybe your heart, whatever feels right. For this ritual, you don't have to speak those feelings out loud, but you certainly can if that's what's calling you. Imagine the jar being filled up with those little bits of energy. Once you feel as though you've released as much as you can, put the lid on the jar.

Speak out loud:

> *My feelings have been released into this vessel,*
> *allowing my mind and body the space deserved.*
> *I honor each of these feelings,*
> *especially as they no longer live solely inside of me.*

The first portion of the ritual is complete. Make sure to stretch and move your body, noticing where you are less tense than before. Reassure yourself that the work you just did had an effect.

Now you have a jar full of released feelings and you need to decide how to complete the spell. For this, you will choose an element. This element will determine what you will do with the jar. Use your intuition to pick an element, but in general, choose the element that represents what you would like more of. For example, if you want more stability, choose earth. More passion, choose fire. More healing, choose water. More inspiration, choose air.

If you choose water, bring your jar to a body of water, opening it and letting the imagined contents pour into the water, knowing the water will bring you peace.

For earth, open your jar and pour it into a small hole in the ground, knowing that the earth will give you grounding.

For fire, open your jar and pour it onto a fire, either a candle flame or a fireplace, knowing the fire will burn up the old and bring you passion.

For air, open your jar in the wind, knowing the air will carry away those feelings. (If you're doing this one, always make sure you're not against the wind, as you don't want the energy in the jar to go right back to you.)

Take a deep breath and say,

> *So be it.*

EXTERNAL WOMB BEDTIME RITUAL FOR COMFORT AND PEACE

This bath ritual is designed to create an environment that comforts you like the womb might, to create peace, slow down racing thoughts, and prepare your mind and body for a restful night's sleep. I notice that it helps with anxiety, depression, and mania alike, though the process will feel different depending on your starting point. This is also a great ritual for insomnia.

What you need:

- Epsom salt
- essential oil of choice (optional, lavender is always a good choice)
- candles
- herbs for smoke cleansing (cedarwood, sage bundle, palo santo, dried rose, incense, etc.)
- plenty of water to drink
- pillow mist (optional)

First, prepare your bed. Freshly cleaned sheets are ideal. Make sure you have all the blankets and pillows you need to feel truly comfortable.

Run your bath to your temperature preference, adding plenty of Epsom salt and your essential oils if desired. Smoke cleanse both your bathroom and your bedroom. To do this, simply burn your cleansing herbs such as cedar, sage, pine, and lavender, letting the smoke purify the energy in your space. Leave a window open while the herbs are burning so the energy can clear from the room. Make sure all distractions are taken care of. Turn off your phone. Light your candles and do the Elemental Opening Ritual in the bathroom before stepping into the bath. Make sure there are no other light sources except for the candles. Let yourself feel the warmth of the water surrounding you as you sit in the quiet, in the dark, with only the candlelight. Take deep, slow breaths. Allow yourself to sink into your environment. Feel free to trail your fingers in the water, or slowly run your hands up and down your body. Each movement in the water, each trailing touch, is simply a reminder that you are here, in your body, in this womb-like environment. Let all your movements be slow.

Recite slowly:

> I came from the dark waters of the womb.
>
> A place of comfortable void, of warm darkness.
>
> I can return to this place whenever I'd like.
>
> I am held here. I am safe here.
>
> Everything else is slowed. Everything else doesn't matter.
>
> Here, I am with the Great Mother.
>
> And I call on her to hold me and comfort me in her embrace.
>
> Please help me and give me peace.

Watch the candle flames, knowing that they represent you, your soul. Your beautiful light that is held so lovingly in the darkness. Notice how the darkness of the room, of the water, is like an envelope that protects and houses that inner light of yours.

Dip your fingers in the water, then bring them to your forehead, touching it lightly.

Say,

I am held in my darkness.

Pass your fingers over the flame of the candle, then bring them to your forehead, touching it lightly.

Say,

I am held in my light.

Repeat this two times, so you will have done this three times.

Finish with:

So be it/Amen.

When you're ready, get out of the bath and prepare yourself for bed. You can do all your normal bedtime routines, like brushing your teeth, washing your face, etc., but make sure you're continuing with slower movements and very little light. You don't want to shock yourself out of the womb. Make sure to drink water, and if you have a pillow mist, use it generously. Climb into your already prepared bed, ready for sleep, and make sure to pay attention to your dreams.

EASING INTO THE DARK FOR MORE GENTLE TRANSITIONS

For those of us who struggle with depression, the transition from day to night can be one of the hardest times of the day, especially in winter when the days are so short. Since depression is often a lack of fire and warmth, using candles is a good way to ease this transition.

As soon as the sun starts going down, light an abundance of candles, placing them around the room. It's important to do this *before* it gets dark since these candle flames are here to retain the warmth and fire of the day as you go into the night. Seeing the flickering reminds you that there is life still around you in the growing dark, and it pings your guides and guardians to be with you. You'll be surprised at how effective this is. You may want to do this as a daily ritual in the weeks that are particularly tough, and you may notice that even the thought of this ritual is comforting when the sun starts to go down. You can leave the candles burning for as long as you like. You may find you only need the candlelight for thirty minutes, or you may find you feel comforted by the candles for hours. Just make sure to put them out before going to bed. Also, if actual flames are a safety hazard with pets or kids, you can use LED candles or even ambient lamps or salt lamps that cast a warm glow.

This incantation is optional and helpful when you're really struggling. Watch the flames and say out loud:

>Fire is alive.
>
>I am alive.
>
>Fire is inside of me.
>
>It burns strong and long and steady.
>
>And my flame will not go out.

SALT SCRUB AND RITUAL SHOWER TO CLEANSE AND SOOTHE

This is a quick and easy recipe and water ritual for when you want to cleanse yourself of excess energy and purify yourself with water to soothe any mental irritation you may be feeling in yourself, or after you've been around others and can feel their energy on you. It's one of my favorite quick rituals to ease anxiety or obsessive thinking.

It's incredibly easy to whip up a small amount of salt scrub on a whim. You simply need a tablespoon of salt, then something to mix it in. Here are some easy options:

Here are some salt options:

- Celtic sea salt
- Himalayan salt
- Epsom salt
- Hawaiian black lava salt

For the mixer, choose a tablespoon of one of the following:

- olive oil (for a thicker, more moisturizing feel)
- sweet almond oil or fractionated coconut oil (for a thinner, smoother feel)
- body wash or shampoo (for a more sudsy effect)

Here are some optional additional ingredients:

- teaspoon of coffee grounds (for further exfoliation and waking up the skin)
- teaspoon of cosmetic clay such as white kaolin clay or French green clay (for extra purifying)

- drop or two of a fragrant body oil or essential oil you enjoy
- pinch of crushed or powdered herbs such as crushed rose petals (for love and beauty), lemon peel powder (for brightening and cleansing), or lavender (for peace and healing). Use your intuition with what feels good for you.

Mix the ingredients into a small bowl until they become a consistency you can spread over your body. While you're in the shower, apply your salt scrub all over your body, keeping your body out of the water stream or momentarily turning off the water. Make sure you've covered and scrubbed your entire body. As you're doing this, visualize all the toxins, physical and emotional, rising up and being pulled by the salt and oils. I often imagine the toxins as black or red, being pulled up from my tissues and my blood and onto the surface of my skin. You can also imagine your positive earth associations.

Once you've done this, get under the shower stream, slowly turning yourself clockwise in the water as it washes away the salt. Visualize the toxins that were sitting on your skin being washed away down the drain.

As you turn, say,

I am cleansed and purified.

I am cleansed and purified.

I am cleansed and purified.

Amen.

For each full turn you make, you recite, "I am cleansed and purified" three times. I like to do a full three turns, but go with your gut and don't make yourself too dizzy.

BATHING IN THE LIGHT OF
THE SUN AND MOON

One of the easiest ways to engage the fire and water elements for soothing is simply by bathing in their energy while thinking about your positive associations of the elements. Both sunlight and moonlight can feel soothing and regenerative. Sunlight is generally the best choice for struggles like depression and overwhelming down moods since it has a warming effect, while moonlight is generally the best choice for struggles like anxiety and mania since it has a cooling effect.

Simply lay in the light of either the sun or moon. You can be outside in your yard, at the beach, in your bed with the window nearby, or even sitting in your car. Breathe deeply and allow that light to sink into your skin. If you're working with the sun, focus on the feeling of warmth and of the fire drying up and comforting the parts of you that are soaked with sadness. If you're working with the moon, focus on that cooling blue light, letting it slide over you, softening your edges. As you do this, notice if you feel any pain or discomfort in your body. Once you've identified where you feel it, physically tap those areas with your fingertips three times, knowing that you're encouraging an opening for that sunlight or moonlight to enter. As you tap, you can visualize the warm yellow or the cool blue seeping into your pain. The most common pain points will be around your heart, around your stomach, or on your head. You can think of it like you're simply knocking on energetic doorways, allowing the energy to go through those doors and deeper into your body. The sun and the moon will do the rest.

NEW MOON RITUAL FOR NEW BEGINNINGS

This is to be done on the new moon. The new moon represents new beginnings, new projects, new relationships, new endeavors, and also is a good time for working with your darker emotions. All you need to do is hold your object that represents your positive association of water and meditate on your new moon goals, then speak your intentions out loud. I'm going to give a mental health example for this spell to give you an idea, but you can personalize this to your circumstances.

> As I begin this new medication regimen, I call upon the power of the new moon to comfort me and give me strength and patience, and to make this transition as easy as possible on my mind and body. So be it.

Afterward, do something tangible that contributes to your goal. For the example above, you could set a new alarm in your phone that reminds you to take your meds every day.

BLOWING IT AWAY RITUAL
FOR RELEASING OBSTACLES
AND SENDING WISHES

All you need for this ritual is a windy day and a handful of dried rose petals. I like using rose petals because they're one of those universal ingredients that work well for all spells, and they infuse self-love into everything. If you have other dried flower petals you love, or even dried leaves, those will work as well—anything that can crumble in your hands.

Find a spot outside that you enjoy, where the wind is whipping around you. For me, I love finding a spot that overlooks the water or a winding path through a beautiful cemetery. You may even want to keep a small jar of rose petals in your car since these windy moments can come at a moment's notice when you're out and about. For each rose petal, speak out loud either a desire that you have that will contribute to your sense of peace or an obstacle that is in the way of you finding that peace. You can use three rose petals—or you can use fifteen. It's entirely up to you, but make sure to speak out loud the desire or the obstacle with each one. Example: "My insomnia goes away and I'm able to sleep soundly," "My family members get off my back," or "I am able to work through my triggers without an episode." When you're done, crumble the rose petals between your hands.

As they crumble in your hands, say:

> *I give my desires and my obstacles to the power of the wind,*
>
> *To be blown away, to be carried,*
>
> *To have the obstacles transmuted and the wishes granted,*
>
> *By the spirits that travel between the leaves of the trees*
>
> *And the petals of the flowers.*
>
> *So be it, and so it is.*

Open your hands and toss or blow your handful of crumbled rose petals into the wind.

WAXING MOON RITUAL FOR GROWING AND BUILDING STRENGTH

This one is to be done on the waxing moon, as the waxing moon is growing and building toward being a full moon. This makes this moon phase perfect for building healthy habits and growing stronger. All you need to do is hold your object that represents your positive association of water and meditate on your desired results, then speak your intentions out loud. The waxing moon is also a great opportunity to bring in the air element if you feel inspired to since air pushes and grows your energy. The Blowing It Away ritual would be great to use here. I'm going to give a mental health example for this spell to give you an idea, but you can personalize this to your circumstances.

> I call upon the power of the waxing moon to give me the strength
> to continue with my daily meditation and exercise practice, so it
> becomes easier and easier, and so I can reach a place where it has
> a long-term effect on my mental health. So be it.

Afterward, do something tangible that contributes to your goal. For the example above, you could immediately go into your exercise or meditation practice the next day, conceding that even if you don't feel the positive effects immediately, you're intentionally building your practice.

FULL MOON RITUAL FOR RELEASING AND CELEBRATING

The moon is at its peak of energy when it's full, which means that any spell you do during this time will be magnified. I like to think of the energy like a firework; the new moon has lit the fuse and the waxing moon has shot it into the sky, but the moment where the firework explodes is the full moon. It's the pinnacle moment, so your *big* spells will have the most power here. All you need to do is hold your object that represents your positive association of water and meditate on your desired results, then speak your intentions out loud. Because of this firework metaphor, you may also want to bring fire into your ritual by burning the spell once you've read it. I'm going to give a specific mental health example for this spell to give you an idea, but you can personalize this to your circumstances.

> *I call upon the power of the full moon to assist me as I release the older version of myself and step into a more empowered, more confident self. I release the mental anguish and suffering and allow myself to embrace the true power and creativity that my mind and my moods offer me. I choose to embrace my uniqueness as a powerful gift instead of the curse I've felt it was. So be it.*

Afterward, do something tangible that contributes to your goal. For the example above, maybe you want to purge your house of old things that remind you of your old self the next week. Maybe you want to go right into one of your positive habits you're building. Just remember that your actions are always weakening or strengthening your spell.

WANING MOON RITUAL
FOR BANISHING

During the waning moon, we watch the moon disappear as it moves toward the dark new moon. This means that it's the perfect time to rid yourself of things you don't need anymore: bad habits, bad thoughts, unhealthy relationships, etc. All you need to do is hold your object that represents your positive association of water and meditate on your desired results, then speak your intentions out loud. Because it is a banishing moon, you may also want to bring in the earth element by burying your spell after you read it. I'm going to give a mental health example for this spell to give you an idea, but you can personalize this to your circumstances.

> I call upon the waning moon to help me rid myself of my habitual
> self-criticism. I recognize that these thoughts don't serve my
> highest good and I cleanse myself of the idea that I can't have
> self-love in my mental health routine.

Afterward, do something tangible that contributes to your goal. For the example above, you can commit to journaling one nice thing about yourself or one thing you're grateful for every time you start to spiral into self-criticism. You can also ask friends and family to share something nice about you in these times, if you're finding it difficult to get there on your own.

MOON WATER

Moon water is one of the easiest and most powerful magickal ingredients to make. Simply take a jar, glass, or bowl of water, set it out under the light of the full moon, and let the moon charge it. This process allows the energy of the moon to be absorbed into the water. From there, you can use that energy in many ways. You can drink the moon water for powerful cleansing. If you're going to be drinking it, be sure to use distilled or filtered water. You can use it as an ingredient in your other spells, which will make those spells much more powerful since the water will already be full of the magickal energy of the moon. You can also use water from the ocean or a beloved river if you have strong positive associations with it. For an energetic boost or extra healing, put crystals or stones in your water. Types of quartz are always great options. You can also add rose petals for self-love and passion or lavender sprigs for healing and peace.

The power of water, the power of the moon, and the power of fluid emotions can all be employed as part of your mental health routine. Using even one of these rituals monthly will create a shift in your ability to work with your moods and your mental health, building trust in your emotions and increasing flow and intuition. Committing yourself to deepening the ways you express your emotions, creating safer spaces for them, and calling upon other forces to help you will give you more tools to turn to when you're seeking peace and comfort.

CHAPTER 5

Protection Spells for Stability and Safety

As human beings in human bodies, we need to feel grounded into our physical experiences to feel safe and stable in our bodies. Unfortunately, between the demands of modern life and the destabilizing effects of trauma and mental imbalance, disconnection from our bodies is all too common. Body disconnection can present as numbness, lack of pain or pleasure, and feeling like you're watching everything from outside of yourself, but don't fully feel the experience. It can also present as a panicked, anxious state. This disconnection can present differently depending on your relationship and experience with safety.

Living in a world that regularly inspires fear makes it difficult to stay connected to our bodies to the point where we can consistently feel safe. Mass shootings and assaults make us feel unsafe among others. Digital work responsibilities and social media can pull us out of any physical experience we're having within seconds. Pandemics can make us fear our own bodies and health. Climate change can make us fear the safety of our futures, the futures of our children, and the futures of animals and the earth itself. Even negative cultural values can increase the lack of safety. Pervasive homophobia and racism keep people feeling unsafe in their identities. The oversexualization of *everything* contradicts itself by pushing an in-your-body act in such a way that often takes away the safety and autonomy of the body, creating a particularly gnarly complex of dissociation.

Those who have experienced trauma will have learned that they had to dissociate from their bodies as a way to protect themselves and feel safer, so returning to the body for physical experiences will be harder because the lack of safety looms heavy. Even when beginning to connect back into the physical, they may then experience the panic of staying with their body because they know it's not yet a safe place for them.

Because of the complicated nature of safety and stability, most of these spells and rituals are centered on the element of earth. Earth is the element that helps us connect back into our physical bodies, as the earth itself is the physical body of our world. The groundedness and stability of earth are what eases us into the experiences of the physical and makes us feel safe in ourselves and in the world. You'll also find a few rituals working with ancestors since ancestor work is one of the most potent types of earth magick. The earth literally holds the bones of our ancestors, the physical history of their lives, which makes them a powerful force in connecting body and spirit.

Using these spells in addition to the grounding tools and the Elemental Opening Ritual you've been given will help you create safety and stability in your mind and body, which will have a continuous effect on the rest of your world and how you operate within it.

INTO YOUR BODY SPELL

This is a very simple and easy spell to bring yourself into your body and remind yourself that it's a safe place to be. It also helps to open yourself up to experiencing the pleasures of being in a body, and the acceptance of pleasure brings an important layer of safety to your life.

The one thing you need for this spell to work is your imagination. Think about a couple of things that you enjoy about being a human on earth. They have to be very tangible things that you can only enjoy while you're in a physical body. You want them to be as delicious and as comforting as you can. They can be food, massages, hiking, sex, sleeping, parenthood, friendship. They can be anything, but they need to be things you genuinely enjoy. My choices are usually coffee, chocolate, sex, and a beautiful view during a hike.

Once you know your things, you need to either have them present or have physical symbols of them on your altar. So, for me, keeping chocolate on my altar works, or a little jar of coffee beans, or a piece of artwork or item that represents sensuality and sex. This could really be anything for you. If one of your favorite experiences in a physical body is going to concerts, you could have past concert tickets on your altar. You could have a picture of your favorite place you like to go to on vacation. It could be a lock of hair from your child. As long as the positive association is strong for you, it will work.

Whenever you're feeling ungrounded, or feeling like you wish you didn't have to be here on earth anymore, you can use this incantation as you focus on your items. This is helpful after you wake up in the morning, especially if you're an intense dreamer who finds it hard to come back to this world. (This is why my morning coffee is such a ritual for me.) It's also really helpful after a stressful situation when your instinct is to dissociate.

Stand in front of your altar and focus on your items, breathing deeply. Imagine that red tube of light from the earlier grounding exercise connecting into the base of your spine from the center of the earth. That red tube of light is pulling all your energy that has floated too high back down into your body. As that's happening, think about how you can only enjoy those items/experiences while in your physical body. Let it be an incentive for you to ground further. Know that those physical experiences are your reward for being fully present in your body.

Recite this incantation:

I call back all my energy that has drifted from my body into other planes and dimensions.

I call back all my strength and all my power

so it may inhabit my physical body on this physical earth

in this lifetime.

I know that I am here on earth to enjoy and appreciate

the taste and the experience of the Divine

through my physical body,

and I call upon my guides and guardians to keep me safe as I inhabit this body.

I am safe within this body.

I am safe to experience pleasure of all sorts.

I call back all my energy

and feed any excess energy to the earth

so I may be balanced and grounded.

So be it.

You can recite this multiple times to help you quickly shift and help it set in. Sets of threes are always very effective. Make sure to breathe deeply and connect with your objects at the close of your incantation. If you'd like to enhance the effects even more, you can enjoy whatever your item/activity is immediately afterward.

If you struggle with trauma and focusing on your body is too intense or unhelpful for you, you can try reciting this incantation out loud without doing any of the other focused physical work to see how it feels and take it at your own pace.

Another option if you are having an especially difficult time with dissociation or anxiety during times of stress and even reciting the incantation feels too difficult is to try focusing on your physical objects or representations. Describe them out loud to the best of your ability. Describe their color, shape, size, texture—anything that helps you focus on the physical world. This helps with grounding and getting back into your body, even if you're not consciously focusing on the body.

WITCH'S BLACK SALT RECIPE AND RITUALS

This recipe shows you how to create your own witch's black salt. Black salt is incredibly effective for protection, boundaries, and cleansing. I'll show you multiple rituals you can use it for.

What you need:

- wax melts or a candle that drips wax easily

- mixing bowl

- small glass jar with a lid (can be cork or screw-on)

- paper and pen

- sea salt (Celtic, Himalayan, or black lava salt)

- ash from previously burnt herbs and incense

- dried rosemary

- dried cedarwood

- any essential oil blend that feels potent and protective to you (optional)

- one individualized item as a secret ingredient

Set the environment. Light candles if you'd like, play music that inspires protection and fierce boundaries, and turn off your phone. Your focus needs to be solely on this task.

In a bowl, combine your sea salt (I prefer a combination of different types), ash, rosemary, cedarwood, essential oils, and your secret ingredient. The secret ingredient is something that will be personal to you, something that represents protection and fierceness. For me, I like to use ground-up shark teeth since the shark is a fearsome protector of mine and represents forward motion. Maybe your secret ingredient is cayenne pepper since you use it a lot in your cooking to cleanse your system. Maybe your secret ingredient is a drop of water from the ocean if you have mermaid leanings. Maybe you use smoky quartz chips if that's one of your favorite protection stones.

There are no specified amounts given with these ingredients because what is *most* important is that you combine these until it looks and feels right to you. If it feels like it needs more ash, add more ash. If it feels like you need more of your secret ingredient, add more. I cannot tell you the correct amount, for the correct amount changes with each batch and each purpose. Feel it and trust yourself. Have fun with it. This part will make you feel like the magickal witchy creature you are.

As you're combining these ingredients, keep protection and boundaries in your mind. Will you use your black salt for all matters of protection and safety? Will you use it specifically for protection against one person who has been taking too much of your energy? Boundaries with yourself when you're not respecting your own mental health needs? Notice the feelings that come up as you decide how much of your ingredients to use. Notice any small murmurs of power that start to rise in your belly, like butterflies in your stomach or a sense of excitement. Once you have combined your ingredients and it feels right to you, scoop the contents into your jar.

What you do next depends on your use for your black salt. Here are some options for you:

GENERAL PROTECTION

When using your black salt for general protection and future use in multiple rituals, there is nothing left you need to do. Put your lid/cork on your jar and you're good to go. Keep the jar on your altar or somewhere safe and use it as needed for various things. You can sprinkle some by your doorways, you can use this mixture for other rituals and spells, you can carry it with you, and you can simply leave it as a guidepost on your altar to remind you that you are powerful and safe.

PROTECTION SPELL FROM A SPECIFIC THING OR PERSON

When using your black salt for protection from a specific thing or person or even a habit of yours you can't shake, you will need pen and paper, plus the wax melts or a candle. On your piece of paper, you will write the person/thing you need protection from as if the protection is already occurring and the spell is already cooking. For example, your piece of paper might say, "I am completely protected from (insert name) and cannot be harmed by them." Or it may say, "I am completely protected from my previous forms of self-destruction and can no longer be tempted by them."

Tear out your sentence, fold it up, and put it inside the jar with your mixture.

Put on the lid/cork and then use the wax melts or candle to drip wax over the jar. As you do this, recite the sentence you wrote on your piece of paper. This seals the spell and contains the energy. Once sealed, keep your jar in a place where you feel you need the protection. For example, if you are seeking protection from a previous abusive partner, placing the jar on your bedside table may be good. If you are seeking protection from online harassment or social media stress, keeping the jar on your desk by your computer is the best place. If you're seeking protection from self-destructive habits like emotional eating, keeping the jar in the kitchen would be good. Use your intuition. You may even want to carry the jar with you.

The more you see your jar, the stronger your association of protection and safety becomes in your mind, which magnifies your will. You are simultaneously working with divine energies *and* using psychological tools to train your brain. You can even repeat what you've written on the piece of paper when you're feeling threatened and need the extra reminder. At some point, you will feel like the jar has done its job and you can dispose of it respectfully and with gratitude. You may want to do another spell where you break the seal and use the mixture in another way, or you may want to break the seal and put the mixture in a fire or in water or bury it. Don't just toss it—you do need to use the mixture, but it's up to your discretion on how you would like to do that respectfully.

BOUNDARIES RITUAL

When using your black salt for assistance with boundaries, you will need a pen and paper. On this paper, you will write two separate things. First, you will write about the circumstances or examples of how your boundaries have been crossed. You can do it in list form or free-writing form. Focus on specific people who are not respecting your boundaries if that's your concern. This can also include yourself and how you're not respecting your own boundaries. Next, you will write the new and healthy boundaries you are setting.

Tear out both entries, putting them across from each other. Then take your black salt mixture, carefully pouring it out to create a solid straight line that goes in between the two entries, clearly separating them. You can choose to use all your salt or just a portion of it, but make sure the line is strong.

Say out loud,

> I separate the way my boundaries have been disrespected and the way I would like my boundaries to be respected from now on.
>
> No longer can this disrespect cross this line.
>
> The only options are to respect my boundaries or calmly leave.

Sit quietly, visually focusing on this separation. You can do this for two minutes—you can do this for twenty minutes. You'll find that depending on your intentions, it may take different amounts of time.

Once you feel it is complete, say out loud,

> It is done.

Use one hand to sweep the line of salt mixture over into the side with your negative/crossed boundaries. Combining the mixture with this entry gives it an extra protective boost. Gather up the mixture and that piece of paper and bury them in the earth. If you'd like to get deeper with it, you could bury it in a specific spot. For example, if it's your boss who is crossing your boundaries, you can bury the mixture under a bush that stands next to your office building. If it's boundaries for your family, you could bury it by your parents' house. If it's boundaries with your mental health, like nightmares caused by trauma, you can put the mixture into a jar along with some dirt from outside and keep it under your bed. With the entry stating your positive and healthy boundaries, you can choose to either burn it, offering it to the ether, or keep the entry on your altar so you can reference it for extra fortitude.

Also, remember that a spell alone will not make you succeed. When it comes to boundaries, you must verbally express your boundaries when appropriate. If you cannot verbally express them, it is unlikely you will get the behavior to change. These rituals are meant to set you up to call upon your guides and guardians to help you, and to help you strengthen your relationship to your mind and heart to create long-term sustainable change.

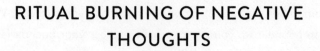

RITUAL BURNING OF NEGATIVE THOUGHTS

This is a really easy ritual for connecting with the fierceness of fire to cleanse yourself of negative thoughts and purge anger. Holding onto those persistent negative thoughts creates a tangled nest in your mind, which activates anxiety and unease. Having that tangled nest makes it all too easy for the uncertainties of life to jump into it and make it worse. Using the transformation of fire can help you eliminate it.

What you need:

- pen and paper
- bowl you can burn things in
- candle

Light your candle. Write down every negative thought that's been bothering you. Don't censor yourself. No one is judging your list. It doesn't matter if they're not even all true. Just get them out. Purge. Don't try to edit your list because you don't want to admit to feeling hate. It's okay to feel it for these purposes. Look at your candle after each one, reminding yourself that fire has the power to burn away and transform. Once you're done, make sure to read your list or thoughts out loud, putting as much of your aggressive energy into them as you can. Get dramatic.

Then it's time to burn it! You can choose to rip it up into pieces or crumple it up before burning or simply torch the entire thing, whatever feels most cathartic. You can also do this with a bonfire. This is a great maintenance ritual to do whenever you feel that buildup of negative loops happening. It helps to release some of those frustrations and uncertainties so you're not spending as much of your mental energy trying to repress those things.

RITUAL FOR HIGH ANXIETY AND MANIA

This ritual is specifically designed for episodes of mania or intense anxiety and helps to bring those moods back down into a place of safety. Being able to do this outside in nature is most effective, but I realize that's not always possible, so there is an alternative version to suit those without that access as well.

Go somewhere where you have access to natural water, whether it's a lake, a river, or an ocean. You'll want to sit down on the ground somewhere that allows you to view the water. Ideally, you'll be able to sit on some big solid rocks, but if that's not available, sitting in the sand or on the dirt works too. You'll want your skin to come into contact with the rocks or ground, so take off your shoes. My favorite place for this ritual is sitting on ancient volcanic rocks in front of Lake Superior.

As you sit, take in your surroundings. Feel the earth beneath you. Feel the texture of it on your feet. Notice the state of the water. Is it calm? Are there waves? What sounds does it create? Is there a breeze in the air? What's the temperature?

Start thinking about what's happening in your body and mind. I know that there's a lot happening. It feels buzzing. Unstable. Like too many things are happening at once, and you can't get a solid focus on any of them. Imagine all those things being pulled up out of your skin and down toward the rocks. You can imagine them like little specks of dirt or blinking red dots. Imagine the earth beneath you eating them up. While this is happening, keep watching the water as it reminds you that the earth and the water are bigger than your mind and what's happening inside of it. You'll begin to feel more and more grounded while you focus on this. You can vocalize what is happening if you'd like, speaking out loud how you're feeling or what the earth is pulling down. This is up to you and where your intention is. I find that speaking out loud what I wish to happen makes the magick much more effective, so you can say something like, "The earth is drawing down all my excess mental energy, connecting and grounding me."

You'll reach a point where you suddenly feel like springing up and taking focused action. It's hard to explain this feeling because it's different with everyone, but it's like this sudden surge of wanting to jump up and shout. It may feel empowering or you may even feel a little anxious, but the point is that you suddenly want to get up and move. This is the moment that the water calls you in. Walk into the water. It works best if you can go completely into the water, submerging yourself and letting the water wash you clean of whatever residue is left on your skin from your visualization. If you can, and if your location is safe, put your head underwater, at least briefly, to catch the excess energies around your head that the earth couldn't pull all the way down. Cold water is best because it awakens your senses and is good for your body as well, but any water is good. If being submerged isn't an option, make sure your feet are in the water. Dip your hands in the water and then touch your arms and neck and head.

Come out of the water when you're ready, thanking both the water and the earth. Pay attention to how you feel, in your mind, and in your feet. Feel free to sit on the earth again. You may even want to repeat this practice a few times. Journal about your experience. Taking note of the details will help you develop more of your elemental sweet spots.

Alternate version: If you don't have access to wild spaces, you can sit on the ground outside or even on the floor in your home. Fill a bowl of cold water and set it in front of you—this is the water you'll focus on. Once you've completed the visualization above, dip your hands in the water then touch your feet, arms, neck, and head. Or bring your bowl of water into the shower with you and pour it over your head.

SAFE IN MY BODY RITUAL

This ritual is very simple, but very powerful for those who struggle with dissociation and trauma. Find a place where you feel comfortable. Maybe it's snuggled up in your bed. Practice deep breathing as you move through this ritual. All you're going to do is move your hands over your body, stopping to focus on specific body parts. For example, move your hands along your arms, focusing on your arms.

As you do this, say out loud:

I am safe in my arms.

Then move to another body part. Maybe your hips. Hold your hips and say:

I am safe in my hips.

Continue to do this with all the parts of yourself. You may find it's a very emotional process for you, and if that's the case, allow yourself to experience your emotions freely.

When you finish the ritual or have done as much as you can handle, close the ritual by saying:

I am safe in my body. Amen.

CLAY FACIAL MASK FOR CLEANSING THE SENSES

Clay masks are a really fun and easy way to connect to the earth and water elements since you're literally slathering them onto your face. Your face also houses so many of your senses that I find it's helpful to consciously cleanse the skin around them. You can find most of these items at natural food stores.

What you need:

- teaspoon of any type of facial clay such as white, rose, bentonite, or French green clay

- activated charcoal powder (optional)

- few drops of frankincense essential oil (optional)

- makeup brush

In a bowl or in your hand, combine your ingredients and add just a tiny bit of water, mixing it thoroughly. You can also use a prepurchased mask if you don't want to purchase the ingredients. Apply the mixture to your face with a paintbrush or designated makeup brush. Using a brush instead of your hands is important because you'll notice how luxurious it feels when you paint the mask on. Let it sit for 5–8 minutes. Add a little water to your face and scrub gently before rinsing off to exfoliate properly. I prefer using cold water because it livens me up and closes my pores, but use whatever temperature feels right. The charcoal and frankincense are a particularly cleansing combination for your skin. The task of exfoliating your face and rinsing away the dead skin cells and dirt is an incredibly simple cleansing ritual, especially considering how our skin can hold a lot of toxins and is particularly vulnerable to the elements.

OFFERINGS TO YOUR ANCESTORS

One of the easiest ways to give your ancestors offerings is by giving them their own plate of food when you eat your meals, usually put outside your door. Many people have specific altars for their ancestors in their homes as well, with family heirlooms and photos. You can also put the offering plate there or make more specific offerings to your loved ones with their favorite food or drink. It is important to talk freely with your ancestors. You may use pre-written incantations if you would like, but I find that it is much more effective to speak from the heart, and even speak very informally and casually. Have conversations with your ancestors. Give them little snippets of updates. Ask them for help. Remember that while you want to honor your ancestors, you don't want to put them in the position of deities. Every lineage comes with its own mixture of good and bad influences, so it's important to remember that in how you work with them. Use respect but also discernment.

When everything in the world feels unstable and unpredictable, knowing you can connect to your ancestors at any time can offer you one element of stability.

OFFERINGS TO THE ANCESTORS
OF THE LAND

It's a sign of great respect to make offerings to the ancestors of the land. Make sure to do your research to figure out who originally inhabited the land you live on so you know who is receiving your offering. Find a spot on the land that feels like a natural altar. This can often be a specific tree or stone; regularly leave your offerings there. If you're not sure where to start, tobacco or food is always a good offering. The spirit in which you offer is much more important than the offering itself, especially when you likely live on land that was stolen from Indigenous people.

Make sure to approach your offerings with complete respect, especially if you are not a part of their spiritual tradition, but that you honor what was theirs and their presence in your life. Make clear that you are open to receiving wisdom and advice on how to honor them and the land better, but do not make demands of them. Constantly use this exercise to examine your cultural privilege and what you do with it. To take your offering further, make sure to share the voices of the Indigenous when it comes to these matters, support businesses or ventures that lift them up, and spread awareness with others when you can.

Using these practices can help you take steps in cleansing and purifying your connection to the earth, which has likely been marred by generations of violence and colonization. This has a ripple effect on your entire mental landscape and increases your personal sense of safety and stability. When you interact with the land differently, you automatically interact with your body differently as well.

RITUAL FOR BREAKING ANCESTRAL PATTERNS

This ritual is good for working with the intergenerational trauma from your lineage and the patterns and imbalances that have been inherited. It's particularly effective for cases of complex post-traumatic stress. It is never a one-and-done spell since intergenerational trauma is very complex and spans across lifetimes. Have patience and know that the work you do is important.

What you need:

- yarn or twine of 3 different colors

- tape

- pen and paper

- scissors

- bowl that's safe for burning things in

- candle or lighter (a long lighter is best)

- family photos or records (optional)

- dried herbs such as cedar, pine, sage, or lavender (optional)

Take your three different colors of yarn or twine. Choose one color for the past, one color for the present, and one color for the future. Cut very long pieces, at least a few feet each. Knot them together at their ends and then tape the knot on a table to hold it steady. Begin to braid the three colors of yarn or twine and meditate as you do this. Have family photos, records, and significant items strewn about the table to reinforce your focus and awareness. Know that as you are braiding, you are drawing your awareness to how the past, present, and future all come together in your family's lineage. Think about what you know about your ancestors, the lives they lived, and everything you *don't* know about them. Think about your family in your life in the present, what you know about them, how they affect you, the family patterns you've experienced. Think about the trauma you've witnessed that maybe your parents and grandparents have as well. Have there been shared experiences of sexual abuse? Have there been shared experiences and patterns of anger? Does depression or anxiety or bipolar disorder run in your family?

As you braid, think about how all those complicated things come together to create the unique being that is you. Think about how your existence continues the tradition into the future through your other family members, your children, or the work you do in the world. The reason I told you to use long pieces of yarn is because I want you to take your time, so you have enough time to reflect on these things and how they're all interwoven together. Once you reach the end of your yarn, tie a knot in the bottom.

Then it's time to make a list. Make a list of known family names, known family patterns such as alcoholism, depression, or sexual abuse, and known patterns that are from your immediate family such as disapproval, guilt, or emotional expectations you cannot meet.

Take your scissors. What you're going to do is make multiple cuts in your braid to represent the cutting of the ties to your lineage that you no longer wish to uphold. For the first cut, you will cut the braid in half after speaking this out loud:

> I am (insert full name here) *and I cut the ties to the ancestral patterns I no longer wish to repeat.*

I honor and respect those who have come before me and I break the spells.

I am no longer beholden to their karmic plays.

The contracts are null and void.

I am the will and the power.

I break the spells.

Once you've made this initial cut, make more cuts to both halves as you recite a version of this incantation that is specific to the pattern you want to break. You can do this with your entire list. If you're using family names, you can say, "I cut the ties to the ancestral patterns of the (insert surname) clan." Continue cutting the braid as you work down your list. Make sure you are speaking the words with intention and with the mindfulness of the braid you have created.

Once your list is done and your braid is in many pieces, put all the pieces into your burning bowl. You can add your herbs as well. Repeat the first incantation one more time as you hold the bowl in your hands. When you are done reciting, say, "It is done." Light your pieces and herbs on fire and offer the ashes to the earth.

Remember that you are still respecting the good of your ancestors when you do this ritual. This is a ritual of free will and it can be very powerful. You may find yourself feeling much freer upon completion of this spell. Make the conscious effort to make choices that are different from your family's negative pattern to strengthen the spell, and revisit this ritual when you feel the time is right. Know that you are working with layers and layers of ancestral karma and trauma, so be consistent and patient. You will feel the difference.

Working with your grounding tools and these rituals will help you to reconnect to your body and create a sense of stability and safety in your life. Having the support of the elements, especially earth and the support of the ancestors, strengthens the ground you stand on so you can walk the path of your life with confidence.

CHAPTER 6

Love and Creativity Spells for Inspiration and Passion

One of the most tragic parts of mental health decline is how those difficulties completely drain us of passion and purpose. So much of our energy is spent trying to stabilize ourselves, leaving little for the joy that sparks our lives. It can be a tricky code to crack because disconnection from the body and overstimulation of the mind is what causes a lack of creativity and expansion in mental health, and creativity and expansion are some of the most powerful forces to overcome disconnection and overstimulation. Our passion makes our mental battles and triumphs worth it. It drives us and gives us a reason to continue battling, even as modern life or unexpected tragedies derail that purpose.

Fire and air are the primary elements used to spark inspiration, passion, purpose, and creativity. Without these elements, your moods can be depressed and lethargic; working them into your magickal practice helps to balance things out. Since these elements are often spontaneous and fleeting in nature, you'll find that this section reads a little differently. Rituals and spells for creativity and inspiration need to be approached in the same way that creativity and inspiration strike naturally—with quick adaptability and spontaneity. You cannot grip a wish in the breeze if it has somewhere to go to fulfill its purpose. You cannot hold a lightning bolt. You cannot fall in love with the wild wind and ask her to stop for you, for even if she did, she would cease to be what you loved about her in the first place. The wildness that inspires is always moving, and embracing and making the most of the beautiful fleeting moments is the key to working powerful creativity and inspiration magick.

That's why you'll find that a lot of what I write here is meant to be a practice that can be applied quickly and without too much preparation or concern. No matter how disconnected from your body you are feeling, you can take one fleeting moment to call that connection back in. No matter how overwhelmed you are by your life or the unpredictability of it all, you can take that one fleeting moment to spark your purpose. Those small fleeting moments add up and change the way you process and notice things, so it becomes more of a habit to seize the bits of joy you can, no matter the circumstance. These rituals are meant to connect you to your inner passion and spark these fleeting moments.

FIRE DANCING TO SPARK YOUR INNER PASSION

There's a reason the image of naked people dancing around fires is such a pervasive and collective Pagan association. The flames of the fire move as the body might move. Smooth and curling, quick and punctuated. Dancing around a fire is an evocation of that element and all it stands for. In terms of mental health, dancing brings you out of your head and into your body all at once, which makes it one of the easiest ways to shift your energy. You don't have to do it around a fire or with a group of other people to receive the benefits, though. You can use your fireplace, simply light a few candles in your living room, put on your favorite music, and dance around however it feels good. As you dance, you can imagine the flame inside of you, moving with your body and with the music.

WATER SINGING TO CLEAR
CREATIVE BLOCKAGES

Creative expression is just that: expression. Energetically, expression often comes from the throat chakra, as we speak into existence our truths and arts. That's why difficulties with creative expression are usually paired with blockages in the throat, even if your art form is not explicitly vocal. An easy way to clear your throat is to sing. One of the most powerful ways to clear your throat through singing is by singing to the water. Water is the holder of emotion and intuition, and truth emerges through the acknowledgment of that intuition. It is represented by the color blue, as is the throat center. The rulers of the sea, the whales, are masters at vocal expression. And, let's not forget the powerful and inspiring archetype of the mermaid or siren, who casts an enchanting spell every time she sings. Singing to the water has a surprisingly powerful effect on both your throat chakra and your inspiration.

Imagine yourself walking barefoot on the beach, singing to the waves as the wind whips your hair around and the sun sets into twilight in pastel pinks and blues. Imagine yourself dipping your toes in a river, singing a sweet little song as the water sparkles against the stones. Imagine yourself in a canoe in the middle of a calm lake, stars above you, as your voice echoes and carries around you. The beautiful drama in this practice is palpable, and you cannot help but feel the pulse of elemental magick as you try it. You do not have to sing well at all, either. And it doesn't even need to be happy. It just has to feel good for you, whether it's a sad song that releases emotions, or an uplifting one that calls in joy. You will often find me at the water with my headphones in, singing, whenever I need to clear my energy and find my truth again.

WIND WALKING TO RECEIVE INSPIRATION

One of the most effective forms of air magick is simply walking in it. Each time a pleasant breeze kicks up and carries the scents of spring, each time a stormy gust sweeps through and sends the fall leaves into a whirl, each time the wind creates beautiful waves on the beach, inspiration magick is at work. Air is the element of information and communication, so each form of air brings new information and messages. Simply walk outside, keeping this in mind. Pay attention to the sound of the leaves in the trees. I find that listening to the trees talk with the wind is a surefire way to inspire my intuition. I also find that enjoying the wind in my hair is an immense source of comfort and validation for me. I like to think that the wind leaves little secrets in my hair and in the leaves of the trees and I just have to listen to be let in on the secret.

Since each form of air has a different mood, you can take these opportunities to embrace your inner drama and match yourself to the mood. You'll often find me in black boots, dark jackets, and black eyeliner on the gray windy days of fall, listening to some intense instrumentals in my headphones. On a beautiful summer day, you're likely to find me barefoot and in a long dress, without a stitch of makeup on, humming lightly with the breeze. Playing along with the wind like this, playing with your inner sense of drama and imagination, encourages the air element to share its information and inspiration with you.

Simply notice how you feel. What you hear. What you see. What does the wind feel like on your skin? What is its mood, its message? Notice what drops into your head later on in the day or what you feel like doing. Also, pay attention to when you're "full"—we all have a limit on how much wind energy we can take. When you realize that you're full, don't linger. Past that point, it will tire you. You want to take in the right amount of information, not be overwhelmed or exhausted by it.

THE ANTI-GRATITUDE LIST FOR RELEASING OBSTACLES

I'm sure that at this point in our mental health journeys, we all understand the benefits of finding gratitude and making little daily notes of those moments. Gratitude is immensely helpful in both mental health and the magickal arts. However, sometimes when we're really suffering with our mental health, any gratitude we might try to engage with is performative and not fully felt. Sometimes to truly tap into our gratitude, we first need to tap into our anti-gratitude to stir the energy and get it moving, so we may then get into gratitude easier. This is a little ritual that subtly uses the air element of movement, the fire element of actionable anger, and the water element of expression. Think of it like a more intentional, structured version of venting.

All you need for this practice is a pen and paper. Instead of writing a list of things you are grateful for, write a list of things you are not grateful for, things you hate. They can be huge meaningful things or they can be petty little things. (Sometimes the petty things make the most difference since the more we pretend we have no pettiness, the more irritated we end up being since we can't express it.) It truly doesn't matter what you choose to write. Once you have your list, go through each statement, reading them out loud and full of your aggressive energy. Shout them if you'd like. The purpose of this practice is to funnel your aggressive energy into the things on your list so you are quite literally expelling them from your body. Take this practice a step further and do it with friends, setting the rules that after each statement is read, everyone else must whoop and holler and agree with said anti-gratitude statement. It feels great to be able to have a safe space for your anti-gratitude and you'll find your genuine gratitude seeping through almost immediately all on its own.

While this isn't a practice to engage in daily, like you would with a gratitude list, it's an easy way to get your energy moving when you're feeling some negative buildup or feeling like you simply can't genuinely get into your gratitude.

SELF-LOVE SPELL TO INVITE COMPASSION AND COMFORT

This easy charm can be used at any time when you're feeling self-critical or down on yourself and need to bring in more self-love. You can keep it handy in your journal or on your phone and recite it when you need a positive affirmation.

To make this charm more of a ritual experience, all you need to do is create an environment of softness for yourself, focusing on textures that you will physically experience. It could be a bed full of pillows you lie down on. A faux fur blanket. A bathtub full of flower petals. It could involve soft music. It could involve the afternoon sun through your window. Anything in your environment that invites softness. The colors of the heart chakra are green and pale pink, so weaving in those colors using candles or crystals is perfect. Rose quartz is priceless in this ritual, so whether you are simply using the verbal charm or creating an environment for it, holding a rose quartz or placing it on your heart will amplify the energy of self-love. Creating this environment for yourself is a way to establish a connection between the charm and your physical body, which makes this kind of magickal work more powerful.

Recite:

I love myself. Even when I feel unlovable. I love myself.

*I honor myself. Even when I don't understand how that is possible.
I honor myself.*

*I forgive myself. Even when I feel my actions are unforgivable.
I forgive myself.*

*I accept myself. Even when I feel that no one could ever accept
me. I accept myself.*

*I comfort myself. Even when everything in my heart hurts.
I comfort myself.*

I am deserving of love. I love myself.

I am deserving of honor. I honor myself.

I am deserving of forgiveness. I forgive myself.

I am deserving of acceptance. I accept myself.

I am deserving of comfort. I comfort myself.

I am deserving of love. I love myself.

*I call upon all my guides and guardians and the grace and comfort
of the Great Mother to help me to feel and accept this love.*

Amen/so be it/let it be so.

If self-love tends to be a struggle for you, try repeating the charm over and over. Play with the volume and speed of your voice and notice how when you change your voice, the way you experience the words changes as well. Since this spell is all about your own experience with yourself, taking plenty of time to explore the words is part of the work.

FULL MOON BATHING FOR QUICK ENERGY

If you're looking for a zap of energy to move out of lethargy and into inspiration, the light of the full moon will quickly do the trick. You can do this without actually seeing the moonlight, but if you can physically put your body in the moonlight, shining on your skin, the effects are more immediate and powerful.

Simply bask in the moonlight and say,

Charge me as you might charge a precious stone.

Fill me with your vibrance and your life,

Pushing out the weariness and replacing it with your energy.

So be it.

Give yourself a good 10 to 30 minutes lying there peacefully, engaging in intentional breathing, but not focusing your mind on anything specific.

Keep in mind that in the true paradoxical fashion of the moon, this kind of energy is just as likely to energize you as it is to exhaust you. Know that whether you can't sleep at all or you're sleeping more than usual, you still took in the energy of the full moon.

LOVER'S SPELL FOR SEXUAL CONNECTION AND PASSION

Sexual expression can be a very powerful tool for managing mental health. Embodying sensuality and letting sexual energy move through you is not only exhilarating but it can also be a wonderful mental balancer, clearing out the energy you don't want anymore and energizing you with fresh passion. Sexual expression for mental health is by no means a requirement, as everyone's sexuality and needs are unique, but this ritual is for those who would like to give their sex lives a little boost and tap into their sensuality for this purpose. It can be done for you and a partner or partners, or for you on your own. It involves the creation of a cacao potion that you drink.

What you need:

- red or pink rose petals (fresh or dried)
- 2 tablespoons cacao powder
- Pinch of cinnamon
- Pinch of cayenne
- teaspoon honey
- red stone, like red jasper or carnelian
- strand of your hair and a strand of your partner's hair
- outfit you feel sexy in (lingerie, your birthday suit, your favorite outfit, or whatever feels good)
- playlist of music that makes you feel sensual or sexy

Set the mood by wearing your sensual outfit of choice, playing the music you like, lighting candles, or using ambient lighting. Spread your rose petals on your altar. Place the two hairs in the bottom of your empty cup. (Or just yours, if doing this solo.) On the stovetop, heat a cup of milk.

Add cacao. As you do this, recite:

> The depth and drive of the primal.

Add cinnamon. Recite:

> The subtle undercurrents that run through our bodies and nervous systems, infusing vibrations of pleasure into us.

Add cayenne pepper. Recite:

> A dose of burning desire, just enough to draw out our juices.

Add honey. Recite:

> Sweetness in love and in life.

Use a whisk to combine the ingredients as the heat builds. Think only of you and your lover (or you and your own sensuality) as you whisk. Note that as the concoction gets hotter, so does your connection with your lover. Once it's hot enough, pour the drink into your cup, over the hairs. Bring your drink to your altar or comfortable space where you'll finish the spell.

Once at your altar, recite:

> (State your full name)
>
> (State your partner's full name)
>
> I am irresistible to them, and them to me.
>
> My body draws them to me, magnetic and true.
>
> Together we inspire, we love, we create.
>
> We feed one another's souls and fill one another's cups.

Our sex purifies us, energizes us, and creates a pathway of electricity in our bodies that brings pleasure and clarity.

So be it.

If doing this ritual for yourself, the previous paragraph would be as follows:

I am irresistible to the Universe, and the Universe to me.

My body draws it to me, magnetic and true.

Together we inspire, we love, we create.

My soul is fed and my cup is full.

My sex purifies and energizes me.

So be it.

Now sip your potion. Allow it to be a sensual experience. Note the flavors and the heat. You do not have to drink the entire potion, especially if you're a little creeped out by the presence of the hairs. The remaining drink can be poured into the earth. This is optional, but you can also take the hairs from the bottom of the cup and keep them hidden away somewhere safe, ideally close to your bed.

If you are doing the ritual while your partner is physically there, you can make love afterward. If you won't be with them until later, simply recall your spell when you make love. If you are doing this ritual for yourself, feel free to engage in self-pleasure. This activates the arts of your love and pleasure as a means for purification and inspiration, which opens your energy channels and naturally helps to balance your moods.

CORD CUTTING RITUAL FOR CLEANING YOUR CONNECTIONS

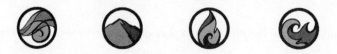

Sometimes, our partnerships and friendships can actually be keeping us from finding more of our natural passion and creativity. We can collect other people's energies, or hold onto mutual stagnant energies, in our minds and bodies. That stagnant energy can turn into blockages that prevent the natural flow of your energy that's needed to maintain your mental health, your creativity, and the inspiration you normally exchange in your relationships. This isn't to say you need to cut off those relationships, though. It's more so to illuminate the need for magickal maintenance. This ritual cleans up those connections and cuts away what isn't needed so what is exchanged within those relationships is healthy and inspiring. You can both use it for a specific toxic connection with a specific person to cut it away entirely and for other connections with others that simply need to be cleaned up.

What you need:

- herbs or incense for smoke cleansing (such as pine, cedar, sage, or palo santo)
- spray bottle of a mixture of water and sea salt
- extra sea salt
- ritual knife or athame (optional but recommended)
- smooth crystal or stone that feels good against your skin

Be sure to heavily smoke cleanse at the start of this ritual, and if possible, keep the herbs burning throughout the entirety of the ritual. I recommend doing the Elemental Opening Ritual before any other ritual, and for more in-depth rituals like this one, it's even more important.

Imagine that every relationship you have with someone manifests as an energetic presence in or around you. These often come in the form of energetic cords, connecting you to another. They can also come in the form of little pieces of energy that were placed into your energy body, almost like people were littering in your aura. Engage in deep breathing as you use your imagination and intuition to feel or see or sense these cords and pieces. You may find that you can actually sense the details of these, and see who each one is connected to, but it's entirely fine if you don't. Knowing they are there is enough for this ritual.

Recite:

> I clear myself of all foreign energies.
>
> I cut the cords of codependence, of emotional and mental drains in my relationships, and of the negative patterns I have with others and that others have with me.
>
> I clear away all the little pieces from others that block my creativity and my emotional flow.
>
> As I cut away all that no longer serves, I make more room for the healthy flow and inspiration I find in my relationships.

Take your ritual knife or athame, or use your hand. A ritual knife is simply a tool you designate to be used for sacred purposes only. If using a ritual knife, keep obvious safety rules in mind and watch where you're moving it. If using your hand, it should be straightened and firm, as if it can slice. Begin to move your knife/athame/hand in quick bursts around your body, a few inches from actually touching you, like you are chopping vegetables. Imagine that your athame or hand is cutting away all the excess or unhealthy ties you have with others, all the cords, and imagine it is clearing all the little pieces stuck in your aura. As you do this, breathe quickly, each exhale in sync with each chop, using your breath to push your energy out, giving more power to your motions. Move your athame all around your body, still in quick bursts and chops, to get all of the hiding energies.

You will likely begin to feel a sticky film forming on your hands as you do this. This is the energy that's being cleared. It's amazing how quickly you'll be able to physically feel it. Because of this, you'll want to regularly spray your hands and your ritual tool with the salt-water mixture as a way of cleansing as you go. Imagine all that energy being purified and going into a beautiful violet flame, which transmutes it into something good.

Continue with the bursts of motion, the quick breaths, and the periods of salt-water cleansing in between. You may find that there are points in your body that require more detailed attention. In these spots, you can slow it down, bringing your tool closer to your body if necessary and focusing your intention on those specific spots.

Do this for at least 3 minutes, but no longer than 10 minutes. It is intense work, and a lot happens in a short amount of time. Afterward, take the smooth stone or crystal and run it over your body, actually touching your body, especially in the areas where you felt the most energy moving around. For the stone, I recommend selenite, but you can choose what you're drawn to. This is like energetic aftercare. Once complete, make sure the knife or your hand has been salt-water cleansed and you smoke cleanse one more time.

Say:

So be it/amen/let it be so.

Immediately after the ritual, use the extra salt you have to thoroughly scrub your hands under running water. If possible, taking a shower using a salt scrub is ideal. Notice how you feel afterward and take it easy. Keep in mind that whenever you do energy work and ritual that removes energy that is attached to you, you may notice a void where it once was. It's common to be tempted into reengaging with the unhealthy connections you cleared or to have those people unconsciously notice that void as well and reach out to reengage. This may manifest as the person contacting you, trying to pull you into old dynamics again, or sudden invitations with those people. Work on your mental health routines instead, focusing on your creative expression, nutrition, movement, your work with your mental health team, and your goals. Because of the intense effects and the importance of soothing and integration afterward, don't use this ritual more than once a month.

All these practices create opportunities to spark creativity and joy in places that may be blocked from or drained of these energies. When our mental health suffers, our passion dies. When our passion dies, our mental health suffers. By working with all the elements, especially fire and air, we can tap into a new flow of purpose and inspiration to help us break that cycle. Being able to use practices that acknowledge the fleeting moments of joy promises new life and motivation amid disconnection, overstimulation, and the chaos and unpredictability of life. Passion and purpose are what make it worth it, no matter how big or small that morsel of purpose is, no matter where it might come from.

CHAPTER 7

Create Your Own Spell

Every ritual and spell in this book can be done as written or can be adjusted for your own needs and moods. When you start feeling comfortable practicing, you can begin to craft your very own rituals and spells. The more you realize that *you* are the main ingredient in your magick and you *are* the magick itself, the easier it becomes to be the creator of your practice and let all the details and elements build themselves around you.

To make this easier, I've created a seven-step template to create your own ritual. I'll go into detail with each step and then give examples for a simple ritual and a more complicated one, and also show you what it would look like to perform them.

Step One: State Your Intention

The more solid you feel in your intention, the more solid your ritual will be. Any sense of wavering intention will make it harder for your spell to work. Write out your specific intention. I always prefer mine to be one to three sentences. Anything longer than that becomes cumbersome and harder to hold in your mind. Take some time to work on this. You want it to be simple and specific. You also need to be able to memorize your intention so it stays with you as you work. Always use present tense when writing out your intentions (i.e., use "I am" instead of "I want" or "I wish"). Write it as if your intention is already happening. Refer to chapter 1 for a refresher on intention.

Step Two: Choose Your Primary Element, Secondary Element, and Logistics

Think about your intention, and knowing what you now know about the elements, their meanings, and your personal associations, choose the primary element that fits your intention best. For example, if you're doing a stabilizing spell, earth may be your best choice. Choose a secondary element as well, if it applies. For example, if you're doing a ritual where you want to acknowledge your sadness and find purpose in it, you could choose both water and fire. Choose when and where you'd like to do your spell based on your feelings and your intention. In the daylight or in the dark? Morning or night? Monday or Friday? Full moon or new moon? In your living room or in the woods?

Step Three: Describe the Action and Transformation

What is moving or changing in your ritual? Are you moving from confusion to clarity? Are you igniting a new feeling? Are you eliminating an old feeling? Are you transmuting your anger into creative passion? Are you encouraging growth in a specific emotional realm? Write these down.

Step Four: Translate that Action into Symbolic Gestures with the Elements and Ingredients

First, work with the elements to create a gesture. For example, if your ritual is to ignite a new feeling, that could translate into lighting a candle. If you're encouraging growth or starting a new habit, you could plant a small seed in a little bit of earth and pour water over it. If you're feeling stagnant in your emotions and want to move forward, you could take a bowl of still water and use your fingers or an altar tool to stir it up and create movement before pouring it out. If you're eliminating an old feeling or habit, you can use water to wash it away, blow it away in the wind, burn it up, or bury it. All those apply. The key is choosing which element feels the most relevant and powerful to you. Keep in mind how you saw the landscape of your negative associations and how you transformed it with your imagination into your positive associations. Those transformations can be made into your ritual gestures.

Then, you can choose ingredients you would like to use. There's no right or wrong here. While there are ingredients that are pretty well known, like using roses for love and salt for cleansing and grounding, your definition of your ingredients is what makes it work. I have jars full of both ordinary and strange ingredients I like to use for spellwork. Some of these include: lemon peel (for joy, happiness, a lighter cleansing), snakeskin (for death and rebirth), rose thorns (for protection, boundaries, processing betrayal or pain in love), birch bark (I use this for a lot of things because of its personal meaning to me), crushed shark teeth (for protection and moving forward), dried or fresh rosemary (for ancestral or remembrance magick), and I even have a jar of raven feathers for my deepest magick since the raven is a creature I work with often. You'll find that once you start doing witchcraft, you'll begin to notice and collect ingredients everywhere and start to look at unusual finds as gifts from the universe, like my raven feathers.

You'll naturally begin to adjust your gestures and motions with your intuition. Using a jar or bowl full of collected treasures for your spell is the best place to start, to build your magickal muscles.

Step Five: Speak Out Loud the Significance of the Gestures and Ingredients

For each element and ingredient, though it doesn't matter so much what they are, it matters *why* they are. Why did you choose that ingredient and that action and how does that fit into your intention? If you're comfortable waiting until you do your ritual to speak these out loud spontaneously, that's fine, but until you're confident doing that, write them down beforehand. Really give it some thought. You're going to be speaking them out loud during your ritual because your voice solidifies and reinforces your intentions.

For example, let's say you chose rose petals in your spell. You might write, "Rose petals to give me softness and self-love as I work on myself" and say that out loud as you add the rose petals to your jar or your giant cauldron (bathtub). Let's say you chose a bit of snakeskin for your ritual. You might write, "Snakeskin to encourage the death of my self-criticism and the rebirth of my self-acceptance" and speak that out loud as you add it to your jar. Or if you are choosing to ignite the snakeskin on fire, you might say, "I burn this snakeskin to watch my self-criticism be consumed by the purifying fire so my magickal workings are bound by rebirth." It's up to you. You get to play with it and make discoveries along the way.

Step Six: Additional Incantation or Charm

This step is optional and depends on how you completed the previous step. If what you wrote for the elements and the ingredients feels like it completely encapsulates your intention, and you have nothing left to say, then you may not need additional written charms. Consider this step kind of like a conclusion statement though. It summarizes and wraps up your workings. This is the part you often see in movies, when the witches recite their spell. Contrary to popular belief, your incantation does *not* have to rhyme. In fact, I prefer it doesn't. To me, it feels too campy when it rhymes, and I want it to feel more real and natural.

Your ritual will be the most powerful if you use language that feels good to you. "I banish thee, oh habits of self-destruction, to the recesses of existence, where you shall be transmuted into light so you may no longer harm me." is just as effective as "Get the hell out of here, self-destruction, and change yourself into something that actually helps me, damnit." as long as you feel that intention deeply.

When you recite your incantation, repeat it at least three times. You can even chant it for as many minutes as you desire. I like to repeat my spell for 10–15 minutes, or long enough for me to fall into a sort of trance with it. Ideally, you want to speak it in multiples of threes (3, 6, 9, etc.), but obviously, if you're choosing to speak it for a long time, it's okay to skip the count.

When finished, end with one of these statements:

So be it.

So be it, and so it is.

Amen.

Let it be so.

It is done.

If you choose to forgo this additional incantation step, and your work felt complete with the previous step, you still want to finish by using one of these concluding statements.

Step Seven: Seal Your Spell

When using physical ingredients in a spell or ritual, you always need to figure out what you're going to do with the physical remnants. Leaving them sitting out with no purpose drains the power from the spell and scatters your energy. Finishing your spell requires one more interaction with the elements. To finish with fire, you can burn your entire mixture in a fireplace. You will often use fire from a candle *during* your ritual and the remnants may be ash, so in this case, you'll want to use a different element to finish it. For earth, you can bury or pour the remnants into a hole in the ground. For water, you can toss the remnants into a body of water. For air, you can blow them away or let the wind take them. Repeat your spell ending one more time as you finish ("So be it" etc.).

If you're using a spell jar, however, you also have the option of sealing the jar closed and keeping the jar of ingredients on your altar. I like to seal them with wax, but as long as you have a lid or covering, that will be fine. Keeping your spell jar on your altar once it's been sealed shut can hold the energy in a sacred way that continues to work on you. However, it cannot stay there forever. You'll have to decide at some point what to do with it when you feel the spell is complete, and then finish your spell using the methods above. An example of this would be if you do a spell jar ritual on the new moon and let it gather and build energy until the full moon, and then you release the spell at that time. Sometimes, you may even feel like the spell jar needs a second ritual when you unseal it and finish it.

SIMPLE SPELL
(EXAMPLE)

State your intention:

I let go of feelings of depression and hopelessness.

Choose your primary element and logistics:

Fire, for burning old feelings and igniting hope. I'll do this ritual at night in my reading room where my altar is, and during the waning moon since this is a banishing spell.

Describe the action or transformation:

I am eliminating negative feelings.

Translate into symbolic gestures with the elements and ingredients:

Candlelight is one of my positive fire associations that also feels gentle, so lighting a candle and using that fire to burn my negative feelings that I've written down is what feels good to me. Candles also represent hope to me.

I'll add rosemary to my bowl because it reminds me of family and ancestry.

A pinch of black salt because it adds grounding and protection.

A small rose quartz stone because it reminds me to love myself even when I'm struggling.

Speak out loud the significance of gestures and ingredients during the ritual:

Black salt to always keep me grounded and protected in my magickal workings, and to draw any excess energy of hopelessness into the earth.

Rosemary, to keep my family and my ancestors with me always, and assist me in clearing the ancestral trauma that contributes to my depression.

Rose quartz, to infuse my working with a gentle sort of self-love, the kind that exists even when I'm struggling to love myself on my own.

I release my feelings of depression and hopelessness into the flame of the fire to be destroyed and transformed into something that will give me hope and joy.

Additional incantation or charm:

To keep this one simple, I feel that I expressed everything I needed to in the previous step. So, I'll just finish it with, "So be it."

Seal the spell.

I've chosen earth to finish the spell because I like the idea that I'm burying what has passed, so I'll take my bowl outside and pour the remnants into a little hole in the earth, then say "So be it" again.

COMPLEX SPELL
(EXAMPLE)

State your intention.

> *My past trauma doesn't have a hold on me anymore and I am able to grow into a healthier, happier version of myself.*

Choose your primary element, secondary element, and logistics.

> *Water, because I'm working with so many emotions. Earth, because I'm using it to pull out excess energy. And also, a moment of fire, since I like to use fire a little bit in most rituals. For logistics, I'm choosing in my home, in the afternoon sun, because it makes me feel comforted and warmed, and during a full moon since I want to amplify the power of the spell.*

Describe the action or transformation.

> *Since the action is letting one form of me pass so another can come forward, there is the sense of both burning up and draining out. This fits with my positive fire and negative water associations as well.*

Translate the actions into symbolic gestures with the elements and ingredients.

> *I will use a small white silk cloth to soak up my tears using the Intentional Weeping Ritual, knowing that as I cry, I'm releasing the deeper patterns of those tears. The white is for purification.*

> *Cedar, to burn in the fire and represent a part of me burning and passing.*

A small jar with dirt, black salt, and black pepper in it, because the dirt is grounding and absorbent, and adding the combination of black salt and black pepper feels like a powerful choice to purify emotions and encourage a burning of sorts.

A small black stone and a small white stone, because I want the reminder of contrasts.

Speak out loud the significance of gestures and ingredients as you do the ritual.

I lay out my white cloth that I used for intentional weeping. I say out loud:

A white cloth, to soak up my tears. As I cry, I know I'm releasing deeper patterns of those tears.

I set the jar on top of the white cloth, lid open, and add the dirt, black salt, and black pepper. I say out loud:

Dirt from the earth, black salt, and black pepper, so it can draw out the trauma and absorb the emotions being wrung out of me.

I hold up the sprig of cedar. I say out loud:

A sprig of cedar, so as it burns, it purifies me.

I burn the sprig of cedar, letting the ash and remnants fall into the jar with the dirt.

Additional incantation or charm:

I release my past trauma, letting it pour out of me with the strength and purity of water.

I honor the darkness of this trauma and what it has taught me.

I honor the light within, the light that has always been there and now burns brighter as I release this older version of myself.

I step into a new skin, a new phase, a new adventure, and I continue to grow in happiness as I respectfully say goodbye to what has passed.

So be it.

Seal the spell.

I pour the contents of the jar onto the center of the white cloth. I place a rock from Lake Michigan in the center on top, and then fold up and tie the cloth around it. The next day, this little bundle is thrown into Lake Michigan, the weight of the rock sinking it to the bottom to its resting place. I keep the small stones as a physical reminder of this spell and this intention. I finish with "So be it." (As a friendly reminder, never throw any toxic ingredients into any body of water.)

Use this template to build your personalized magickal practice. Use your personal elemental associations to inform your work. The potential is limitless. If you feel overwhelmed by your options, use this template in its simplest form. Pick one intention, one element, one action, and go from there. Remember, it's not so much *how* you do your ritual or spell, but *why* you do it. Your intentions are what make it work.

Because this is mood magick, you also have to prioritize the way the magick makes you *feel*. Don't be afraid to experiment with your practice, engaging with your imagination and your inner drama and theatrics, noting how those practices affect your feelings. If you are trying a ritual that doesn't feel right to you, or one that didn't make you feel good after doing it (beyond the expected minor discomfort of trying new things or feeling hard feelings), then that's not the one for you and that's okay. If you follow your feelings, you'll discover your elemental powers and your unique spells to reinforce and build your powers as a mood witch.

Conclusion

The state of your mental health is constantly evolving and adapting to your changing environment. Sometimes, the tools you've been using up to this point are everything you need to manage it. Sometimes, though, you need to add some new tools to your belt and expand your repertoire. Witchcraft and the four elements offer you an exciting and magickal way to engage with your mental health and emotional landscape. It's a way to return to our roots, to nature. Our minds are often so overwhelmed and overstimulated with the demands and pressures of a technologically and information-driven culture that we lose our grounding and our connections to our bodies. We weren't made to process that much information all at once. We were made for exploring the world in a sustainable and meaningful way, knowing that the closer we are to the elements, the closer we are to ourselves.

Elemental magick is simple, and yet, it alters your perspective in such a way that your entire life can change. You will no longer passively see the waves on the shore. You will understand that water is the realm of emotion and intuition, and watching the waves kiss the shore will remind you of the innate wisdom of cycles and the transient nature of moods, soothing your insecurities. You will no longer light a candle just because you think it's pretty. You will be reminded of the hope and the passion that you call upon inside of yourself and see the flames dance with life and in recognition of that creative source in your soul. You will no longer simply walk through the woods. You will take your shoes off, letting your skin connect with the stabilizing power of the earth, and understand that you can give her all the excess energies that are stuck inside your body so you may feel safe and protected again. You will no longer ignore a breeze on a beautiful day. You will hear the whispers and secrets of the wind through your hair and in the leaves of the trees and realize that as long as you pay attention and listen, you will be inspired. All the elements will course through you and become a part of you, creating habits that will bring you joy, meaning, and an innate source of wisdom for all the days to come.

As you continue working with the four elements in the ways that feel good to you, I hope you'll come to realize how powerful you truly are, and how precious every part of you is. No matter what you are struggling with, whether it's a situational mental health decline or a lifelong mental illness, those struggles don't have to define you. They don't have to rule you. You can use your moods as magickal fuel to embrace every bit of you, light and dark, good and bad, seen and hidden. There is no shame in experiencing the highs and lows of the human experience, and there is no shame in a brain that operates differently from the perceived norm. Those unique experiences and those unique ways of seeing the world are exactly the things that make *you* the magick itself, and you can use them to shape and better your life and your mind as long as you have the imagination to see it through.

Stay magick, my friends.

Acknowledgments

I've noticed that whenever I embark on a writing project, life throws me conditions in which I need to practice exactly what I'm writing about at the time I'm writing it. Like a friendly reminder from the universe that the teacher should always be learning and practicing. Because of that, I would like to first and foremost thank my mental health support team. The loving influence of Paul, the unending support of my Beloved Coven of Cheyenne, Eleanor and Rae, and the new grounding influence of my local friends, Tina and Erin. All these lovely humans have helped to remind me that my mental health struggles are an important part of me, a part of me to be honored and lifted up.

I always want to shout out my mother, Debra, my father, Patrick, and my stepmother, Jackie, for continuously supporting this strange and interesting life of mine, whether they understand my motivations or not. At least it's not boring, right?

To the team at New Harbinger, who has the uncanny ability to focus my creative whims and ambitions in a way that feels authentic and expansive, and especially to my brilliant editor Jennye Garibaldi, who puts in so much loving work to not only revolutionize the way we work with our own psychology but also to honor my unique role in that as well.

And finally, I am always beyond grateful for the readers. I've made so many beautiful personal connections with all of you over the last couple of years, and knowing that my work can potentially help even one person or make one thing easier on someone makes it all worth it.

Ora North is a spiritual teacher, witch, and mental health advocate. While very involved in the spiritual community, North does not subscribe to the "love and light" or "good vibes only" mentality that can often whitewash or bypass the very real struggles of the marginalized. Because of this, her focus is on shadow work, and promoting the acceptance and validation of all of our feelings—not just the positive ones—as tools for growth. She is author of *I Don't Want to Be an Empath Anymore*.

MORE BOOKS for the SPIRITUAL SEEKER

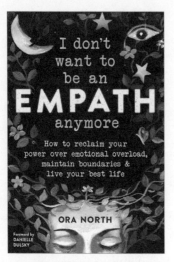
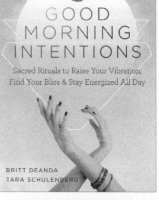
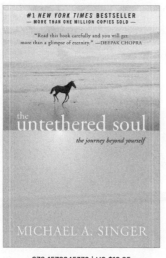
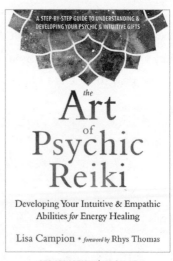